Lawless Tradition

Lawless Tradition

God's Victory Despite Christendom's Failure

P. D. BLACKWELL

Lawless Tradition: God's Victory Despite Christendom's Failure

2nd Edition

ISBN: 978-1-7366096-3-7

Cover design and all interior artwork by: P. D. Blackwell

List of Abbreviations

AAT - An American Translation, 1923, Edgar J. Goodspeed, Public Domain

AMP - The Amplified Bible, ©1987, The Lockman Foundation

ANTB - A New Translation of the Bible, 1922, James A. R. Moffatt, Public Domain

ASV - American Standard Version, 1901, Public Domain

BBE - Bible in Basic English, 1949, Cambridge Press, Public Domain

B.C.E. - Before the Common Era

BES - Brenton's English Septuagint, 1851, Sir Lancelot Charles Lee Brenton, Public Domain

BLE - The Bible in Living English, 1898-1943, Steven T. Byington, Public Domain

C.E. - Common Era

CEV - Contemporary English Version, © 1995, American Bible Society

CPV - Cotton Patch Version, Matthew and John by Clarence Jordan, © 1970 Florence Jordan

ESV - English Standard Version, © 2016, Crossway Bibles

ECT - Eth Cepher Translation, © 2013-2020, Cepher Publishing Group

GNB - Good News Bible, © 1992, American Bible Society

ISV - International Standard Version, ©1996-2010, The ISV Foundation

ISBE - International Standard Bible Encyclopedia, © 1980, Wm. B. Eerdmans Publishing Co.

JPS - Jewish Publication Society Old Testament, 1917, Public Domain

KJV - King James Version, 1611, Public Domain

LEB - Lexham English Bible, © 2012, Logos Research Systems, Inc.

LSV - Literal Standard Version, © 2020, Covenant Press & The Covenant Christian Coalition

LXX - Septuaginta © 1979 Deutsche Bibelgesellschaft Stuttgart

NEB - The New English Bible, © 1976, Oxford University Press, Inc.

NET - New English Translation, © 1996-2017, Biblical Studies Press, LLC

NETS - New English Translation of the Septuagint, © 2007, Oxford University Press

NT - New Testament

NTMS - The New Testament in Modern Speech, © 1929, James Clarke & CO., LTD.

ONT - The Original New Testament, © 1985, Hugh J. Schonfield, Harper & Row Publishers

OT - Old Testament

TCENT - Text-Critical English New Testament, © 2022, Robert Adam Boyd

TEB - The Emphasized Bible, 1897, Joseph Bryant Rotherham, Public Domain

TGNT - The Greek New Testament © 1983, United Bible Societies

TLB - The Living Bible © 1971 Tyndale House Publishers

TMNT - The Modern New Testament, © 1940, George M. Lamsa, A.J. Holman Company

TTNT - The Translators New Testament, © 1973, The British and Foreign Bible Society

WAY -Letters of Paul, Hebrews and the Book of Psalms, Arthur S. Way, © 1981 Kregel Publications

WEB - World English Bible, 2014, Public Domain

WNT - The New Testament in the Language of the People, 1937, Charles B. Williams, Public Domain

YLT - Young's Literal Translation, 1898, J.N. Young, Public Domain

20CNT - The Twentieth Century New Testament, 1904, W.T. Stead, Public Domain

Introduction

The seeds of this book were planted in 1980, while I read commentary about the parable of the wheat and the weeds in the 13th chapter of Matthew's gospel. Here is the parable:

> He put another parable before them, saying, "The kingdom of heaven may be compared to a man who sowed good seed in his field, but while his men were sleeping, his enemy came and sowed weeds among the wheat and went away.
> "So when the plants came up and bore grain, then the weeds appeared also. And the servants of the master of the house came and said to him, 'Master, did you not sow good seed in your field? How then does it have weeds?'
> "He said to them, 'An enemy has done this.'
> "So the servants said to him, 'Then do you want us to go and gather them?'
> "But he said, 'No, lest in gathering the weeds you root up the wheat along with them. Let both grow together until the harvest, and at harvest time I will tell the reapers, "Gather the weeds first and bind them in bundles to be burned, but gather the wheat into my barn."'" —*Matthew 13:24-30 ESV*

A few verses later, Jesus explains the meaning of the wheat and the weeds:

> Then he left the crowds and went into the house. And his disciples came to him, saying, "Explain to us the parable of the weeds of the field."
> He answered, "The one who sows the good seed is the Son of Man. The field is the world, and the good seed are the sons of the kingdom. The weeds are the sons of the evil one, and the enemy who sowed them is the devil. The harvest is the end of the age, and the reapers are angels.
> "Just as the weeds are gathered and burned with fire, so will it be at the end of the age. The Son of Man will send his angels, and they will gather out of his kingdom all causes of sin and all law-breakers, and throw them into the fiery furnace. In that place there will be weeping and gnashing of teeth.
> "Then the righteous will shine like the sun in the kingdom of their Father. He who has ears, let him hear." —*Matthew 13:36-43 ESV*

After reading the parable, I realized my spiritual path would need to surmount obstacles both outside and inside the church, especially after I read the following commentary in the *International Standard Bible Encyclopedia:*

> The tares [weeds] are not wicked men in general, but a particular class of wicked brought into close and contaminating association with the children of God. "Within the territory of the visible church the tares are deposited" (Dr. David Brown). It is the corruption of Christendom that is meant, a gigantic fact to which we cannot shut our eyes. . . Christendom once corrupted remains so to the end.

> . . . In spite of all efforts to correct and reform, the corruption of Christendom remains, nay, grows apace. To expel the vast crop of false doctrine, false professors, false teachers, is now as it has been for centuries, an impossibility. *Orr, James, Editor, 1929, ISBE, 1980 Edition, Eerdmans Publishing Company, Volume 3, Page 2053.*

By allowing the weeds to continue to grow, the church was corrupted.

The lawless corruption within Christianity has been written about in many scholarly works, from Philip Schaff's *History of the Christian Church*, to Max Brod's *Paganism-Christianity-Judaism: A Confession of Faith.* Sir James George Frazer's *The Golden Bough* is an exhaustive work on comparative religion and reveals many of the pagan roots of modern church practices, as does the more recent, *Pagan Christianity?: Exploring the Roots of Our Church Practices,* by Frank Viola.

The corruption of Christendom is a complex subject because non-Christian influences have been part of the Christian experience since the founding of the Church. Some people may be completely ignorant of the pagan roots of church traditions, others may choose to ignore the non-Christian influence because of other motivations, but the pagan influence in the modern Christian church persists.

While pagan concepts have corrupted the biblical perception of God and His purposes, differences between languages have also altered our understanding of various words and phrases in the original documents. Identifying God accurately is important—how can we truly know him if our impressions of him are based in part on pagan theology, and confounded by inaccurate translations? The focus of this publication is to remove the pagan veil obscuring scripture and restore the intended meaning behind the inspired Word of God.

To help with understanding, we will use the name Yahweh when referring to the Almighty Creator. This name is based on the Hebrew יהוה (yhwh), and is the proper name of the God of Israel.

We will also quote a variety of English translations. Some translations confuse understanding due to sentence arrangement (like keeping original language word order that is uncommon in English), or inferior translating based on modern concepts that distort the original intended meaning. Our goal is to achieve accurate understanding. While the main translation used will be the *Lexham English Bible*, we will also use other translations to help express the intended meaning of the authors.

While the parable of the wheat and the weeds is an accurate description of Christendom, true worship is possible. We just need to find the true message contained in the Word of God, and remember the words recorded in Luke's gospel:

> And someone said to him, "Lord, are there only a few who are saved?" And he said to them, "Make every effort to enter through the narrow door, because many, I tell you, will seek to enter and will not be able." *—Luke 13: 23,24 LEB*

—P.D. Blackwell, July, 2023

Part One

Uprooting the Weeds

The following chapters examine scriptural concepts that have been usurped by pagan-influenced theology. By shining light on these forgotten biblical facts, the stranglehold of erroneous doctrine will weaken and fade away.

You will know the truth, and the truth will set you free.
—John 8:32 LEB

Chapter 1

A Cultural and Linguistic Foundation

Culture is the foundation of any society, built upon traditions that are weaved into each generation by those who came before. We are not born with an implanted culture. We are taught by our parents, by our educators, by people in other positions of authority, and by our peers—we learn our culture as we grow. And culture is never static. It is a complex fluid perception, parts of which can change from generation to generation. We experience this change as fashion standards evolve, as popular music shifts from one style to another style. Many of the ancient aspects of culture remain, but there is always a slow shift that represses portions of both ancient traditions and the culture of prior generations—the old become overshadowed by the new.

The changing cultural perspectives of each generation have played an important role in the evolution of Christianity. These changes are like what happened to the religion of the Hebrews. What began with Abraham circa the 20th-century B.C.E., and was formalized by Moses in the 15th-century B.C.E., morphed by the 1st-century C.E. into multiple flavors of Judaism. While the Mosaic Law was still the foundation of their formal worship, the generational changes through history made the first-century religion of Yahweh a collection of diverse religious interpretations that were similar, but different.

> It cannot be denied that the religion of Israel passed through many changes. It grew and purified and spiritualized itself out of its own inherent strength; but it also suffered many relapses, when hindering and corrupting influence gained the upper hand. *Orr, James, Editor, 1929, ISBE, 1980 Edition, Eerdmans Publishing Company, Vol.3, Page 1541.*

Alterations to the Christian faith have produced the multi-denominational Christendom of the 21st-century; a conglomerate of diverse interpretations, unrecognizable when compared to the 1st -century original.

Our understanding is influenced by current cultural norms (as when scripture is read with a modern outlook), but also by translations from the original languages of the Bible. Languages are also not static. Words used to translate a specific meaning hundreds of years ago, may imply something entirely different in current vocabulary that was not intended by the original author.

An example of this change in meaning is found in the seventh chapter of the first letter to the Corinthians. Paul discusses principles for marriage. In verses 7 through 9, he discusses the gift of singleness and his preference for the unmarried and widows (my comments in brackets).

> 7. For I would that all men were even as I myself [Paul was not married]. But every man hath his proper gift of God, one after this manner, and another after that.
> 8. I say therefore to the unmarried and widows, It is good for them if they abide even as I [as unmarried Christians].
> 9. But if they cannot contain, let them marry: for it is better to marry than to burn. —*1 Corinthians 7:7-9 KJV*

There is much we can say about each of these verses, but for now we will focus on verse 9. The Greek word in verse 9 translated "let them marry," is γαμησάτωσαν (gam-ĕs-áh-tō-sahn), the aorist, active, imperative, third person plural of the root γαμέω (gam-ĕh-oh), "I marry." The King James translators, because of the imperative nature of the meaning in Greek, translated the word "let them marry" because "let them" is a third person imperative phrase in Early Modern English (1500 C.E. to 1700 C.E.), and thus corresponds to the Greek imperative tense. Many readers today take the phrase "let them" to mean "allow them," which is not as forceful and removes the imperative intent behind the original word. This has prompted some modern translators to change the English words in this verse to better reflect the original contextual meaning.

> However, if they cannot control themselves, they should get married, for it is better to marry than to burn with passion. —*1 Corinthians 7:9 ISV*

This type of linguistic shifting in English is a minor bump on our path to understanding scripture. Other cultural and linguistic differences between Hebrew and Greek are much more detrimental, and have influenced our understanding so severely that recovering from the corrupt theology can be an impassable hurdle for many Christians; Impassable because the cultural and linguistic misunderstandings have been piling up for almost two thousand years, making that hurdle extremely high.

Repeat a corrupt understanding long enough and it will morph into an accepted truth by the majority, changing forever the author's original meaning.

The centuries of corruption embedded in modern Christianity is our number one obstacle to worship the Father in spirit and truth.

> But a time is coming—and now is here—when the true worshipers will worship the Father in spirit and truth, for the Father seeks such people to be His

> worshipers. God is spirit, and the people who worship him must worship in spirit and truth. —
> *John 4:23, 24 NET*

The first step to remove the obstacles to our understanding is to read scripture with the same frame of mind as those to whom it was written. This is easier than one may think, but demands we toss away all modern perspectives and rely on the text to inform us of the intent behind the scripture. To do this successfully, we must:

1. Learn to recognize ancient metaphors and idioms used by the authors.
2. Understand the authors of the NT had a perspective built on a deep foundation of Hebrew literature.
3. Allow context to determine meaning.

While it is not essential to have a knowledge of ancient languages, we will examine information from lexicons and other resources to help glean the intended meaning of scripture. The context will shape our understanding, allow us to identify all obstacles, and guide us toward accurate meaning.

Chapter 2

Understanding God

The word *god* in Modern English has a variety of meanings.

1. The all-powerful, all-knowing creator of the universe, worshiped as the only god.

2. A supernatural being: one of a group of supernatural beings, each of which is worshiped as the personification or controller of some aspect of the universe.

3. A figure or image: a representation of a god, used as an object of worship.

4. Something that is so important it takes over somebody's life at the exclusion of everything else.

5. Somebody admired: a person widely admired or imitated.

Words with multiple meanings require awareness of the surrounding context to understand what the writer intended to relate.

The most widely distributed terms for *god* in Hebrew are אל, *el,* אלהים, *elohim* (plural), and אלוה, *eloah* (singular). The title אל, *el,* is frequently combined with nouns or adjectives to express particular attributes like אל שׁדי, *El Shaddai,* (God Almighty), אל עליון, *El Elyon,* (God Most High), and is found in Hebrew proper names such as אלישע, *Elisha* (God is salvation), אלעזר, *Eliezer* (God has helped), דניאל, *Daniel* (Judge of God), and מיכאל, *Michael* (Who is like God).

El, elohim, and *eloah* are terms used for members of the deity class. They may also denote honor and authority among men. Therefore, context is just as important as it is in English to discern the intended meaning, because these words are used throughout the OT to identify different individuals.

1. Divine Ones, Superhuman Beings

a. Yahweh, the God of Israel. "And *God (elohim)*[1] said again to Moses, "So you must say to the Israelites, 'Yahweh, the *God (elohim)* of your ancestors . . . has sent me to you.'" —*Exodus 3:15 LEB*

b. Angels. ". . . what is a human being that you think of him? and a child of humankind that you care for him? And you made him a little lower than *heavenly beings (elohim)*." —*Psalm 8:4,5 LEB* (Compare Hebrews 2:6,7)

c. The *elohim* of Yahweh's heavenly council. "*God (elohim)* stands in the divine assembly; he administers judgment in the midst of the *gods (elohim)*." —*Psalm 82:1 LEB*

1. The plural, *elohim*, is the most frequent form used, often with singular verbs and adjectives. Different explanations have been proposed for this, but in the OT this construction only signifies the general notion of deity. See *ISBE*, Vol 2, page 1254, The Names of God.

2. Rulers, Judges, as Divine Representatives

> Moses was *elohim* to Pharaoh. "And Yahweh said to Moses, 'See, I have made you as a god *(elohim)* to Pharaoh, and Aaron your brother will be your prophet.'" —*Exodus 7:1 LEB*

3. A god or goddess: The gods of foreign nations.

> ". . . and went and served other gods *(elohim)* and worshiped them, gods *(elohim)* whom they had not known and whom he [Yahweh] had not allotted to them." —*Deuteronomy 29:26 ESV*

4. Wicked Spirits.

> "They sacrificed to the demons, not God *(eloah)*, to gods *(elohim)* whom they had not known, new gods *(elohim)* who came from recent times; their ancestors had not known them."
> —*Deuteronomy 32:17 LEB*

The individuals mentioned in the scriptures above have one thing in common: they have a connection to the spiritual realm. Yahweh, the lesser gods, angels, and demons, are all inhabitants of the unseen spiritual realm; Moses held a special place of authority among humans and had a unique spiritual relationship with Yahweh.

Yahweh is one of the *elohim* because he lives in the spiritual realm, but no other *elohim* is Yahweh. Yahweh is not one among equals; He is unique.

> There is none like you among the gods *(elohim)*, O Lord,
> and there are no works like yours. —*Psalm 86:8 LEB*

> "And to whom you will compare me, and am I equal?" says the holy one. . . Have you not known, or have you not heard? Yahweh is the God *(eloah)* of eternity, the creator of the ends of the earth!
> *—Isaiah 40:25, 28 LEB*

> There is none like you, O Yahweh, you are great and your name is great in might. *—Jeremiah 10:6 LEB*

> Then Solomon stood before the altar of Yahweh in the presence of all of the assembly of Israel, and he spread out his hands to the heavens, and he said, "O Yahweh, God *(eloah)* of Israel, there is no god *(elohim)* like you in the heavens above or on the earth beneath." *—1 Kings 8:22, 23 LEB*

In summary, the words אל, *el,* אלהים, *elohim,* and אלוה, *eloah* identify multiple individuals. The classification of all those in the spiritual realm as *elohim* was an integral part of Hebrew theology. Yahweh is always the incomparable Creator, the deity with no equal, while the other *elohim,* whether heavenly beings or humans, were created and exist by Yahweh's will.

> Praise Yah! Praise Yahweh from the heavens! Praise him in the heights! Praise him, all his angels! Praise him, all his army! Praise him, sun and moon! Praise him, all you shining stars! Praise him, you heavens of heavens, you waters that are above the heavens. Let them praise Yahweh's name, *for he commanded, and they were created. —Psalm 148:1-5 WEB (emphasis mine)*

Both the English and Hebrew words for *god* are not proper names. Titles like King, Manager, and Overseer fall into the same category of noun as the words for god; they are descriptive terms that emphasize attributes or rank among a select group of individuals.

Chapter 3

θεός: the Greek God

From the *International Standard Bible Encyclopedia:*

> The variety of names [for God] which characterizes the OT is lacking in the NT, where we are all but limited to two names, each of which corresponds to several in the OT. The most frequent is the name "God" (θεός, thĕ-ŏs) occurring over 1,000 times, and corresponding to El, Elohim, etc., of the OT. . . in its true sense it expresses essential Deity. *Orr, James, Editor, 1929, ISBE, 1980 Edition, Eerdmans Publishing Company, Volume 2, pages 1267, 1268.*

While the scholarship of the *ISBE* is commendable, it is also plagued by tradition-bred assumptions, which is evident by referring to *thĕ-ŏs* as a *name.* While *thĕ-ŏs* is used to translate e*l,* e*lohim* and other Hebrew words for god, like the English and Hebrew words, *thĕ-ŏs* is not a proper name, it is a descriptive term; a title used to identify a specific quality held by individuals, whether gentile gods or Hebrew gods.

Because options for translators are limited when choosing words for *god* in Greek, we should not assume the classical use of the Greek word *thĕ-ŏs* is adequate to fully encompass the original meaning of the words transcribed in the Hebrew scriptures. Once again, context should rule our deductions regarding the writer's intent. Also imperative to our understanding is the writer's frame of mind; worshipers of Yahweh will carry with them their foundation in Hebrew theology as they present Christian revelations. Although hampered a bit by the limited Greek verbiage used to translate the Hebrew meaning, the reality of the spiritual realm did not change from the OT to the NT, and most important, the Almighty God did not change.

> For I, Yahweh, have not changed. —*Malachi 3:6 LEB*

> Every good gift and every perfect gift is from above,
> coming down from the Father of lights, with whom
> there is no variation or shadow due to change.
> —*James 1:17 ESV*

What is Deity?

The *ISBE* states that *thĕ-ŏs* "expresses essential Deity." Here are the things the English word *deity* is used to identify:

1. A god or goddess, or other being regarded as divine.
2. Divine state: the condition or status of a god or goddess.
3. Somebody or something resembling god: somebody or something that is treated like a god.

Once again, we have a word with multiple meanings that is applied to more than one individual. Similar to *elohim*, deity (being divine) is a quality limited to specific individuals who have access to the spirit realm.

The understanding that being divine does not make one equal to Yahweh is emphasized when we read from Peter's second letter:

> His divine power has granted to us all things that pertain to life and godliness, through the knowledge of him who called us to his own glory and excellence, by which he has granted to us his precious and very great promises, so that through them *you may become partakers of the divine nature*, having escaped from the corruption that is in the world because of sinful desire. *—2 Peter 1:3, 4 ESV* (*emphasis mine*)

If faithful Christians will become "partakers of the divine nature," then divinity is not limited to Yahweh. Divinity must refer to a state of existence different from what is now experienced in the physical world, because the faithful will have "escaped from the corruption that is in the world."

Because divinity refers to those who live in or have a connection to the spirit realm, a biblical *thĕ-ŏs,* who "expresses essential deity," must also exist in a state beyond our current worldly existence. Yet having the title, *thĕ-ŏs,* cannot express equality to the Almighty Creator Yahweh, because he is unique among all heavenly beings.

> For you, Yahweh, are most high above all the earth. You are exalted far above all gods *(elohim). —Psalm 97:9 WEB*

θεός: The Word That Caused Confusion

The Greek word *thĕ-ŏs,* more than any other term, helped alter Christian theology. We have seen *elohim* and *thĕ-ŏs* are titles and not proper names, and like the English word *god,* they identify qualities inherent in the person identified, and are applied to multiple individuals throughout scripture. One reason for the pagan shift in Christian theology, is how the word *thĕ-ŏs* is used in the Greek scriptures in connection to the Messiah, and misunderstood by gentile converts to Christianity.

Deity, or being divine, is a quality held by those labeled *thĕ-ŏs.* Even that original serpent, the one called Devil and Satan, is called *thĕ-ŏs*:

> . . . the god *(thĕ-ŏs)* of this age[2] has blinded the minds of those who do not believe so they would not see the light of the glorious gospel of Christ, who is the image of God *(thĕ-os). —2 Corinthians 4:4 LEB*

We must take care to discern the subject of the title; is it Yahweh or someone else? In the above scripture the first use of *thĕ-ŏs* is part of the phrase, "the god of this age," ὁ θεὸς τούτου τοῦ αἰῶνος, (hŏ thĕ-ŏs toú-tou toũ ai-ōn-os), which identifies someone other than Yahweh. The immediate context points to the Devil:

> But even if our gospel is veiled, it is veiled only to those who are perishing, among whom the god of this age has blinded the minds of those who do not believe so they would not see the light of the glorious gospel of Christ. *—2 Corinthians 4:3,4 LEB*

In the greater context of other New Testament writings, Satan the Devil is identified as being the ruler of the world; hence the god of this world.

> We know that we belong to God even though the whole world is under the rule of the Evil One. *—1 John 5:19 GNB*

---

2. The word translated "age" in the *LEB* is often rendered "world" in other translations, and is an acceptable alternative. Like many Greek words, context helps determine meaning. The word αἰῶνος (ai-ōn-os), defines an age; a cycle of time; by implication in 2 Corinthians 4:4, the present world of humankind ruled by Satan; or as in Matthew 24:3, the age of the Mosaic Law.

And he [the devil] led him [Jesus] up and showed him all the kingdoms of the world in a moment of time. And the devil said to him, "I will give you all this domain and their glory, because it has been handed over to me, and I can give it to whomever I want. So if you will worship before me, all this will be yours. —*Luke 4: 5-7 LEB*

Now is the time for the judgment of this world to begin. Now will the ruler of this world be thrown out. —*John 12:31 ISV*

I will not talk with you much longer, because the ruler of this world is coming. He has no power over me. —*John 14:30 ISV*

The ruler of this world has been judged. —*John 16:11 ISV*

Then the end will come, when after he has done away with every ruler and every authority and power, the Messiah hands over the kingdom to God the Father. —*1 Corinthians 15:24 ISV*

Put on the full armor of God, so that you may be able to stand against the stratagems of the devil, because our struggle is not against blood and flesh, but against the rulers, against the authorities, against the world rulers of this darkness, against the spiritual forces of wickedness in the heavenly places. —*Ephesians 6:11,12 LEB*

You used to be dead because of your offenses and sins, that you once practiced as you lived according to the ways of this present world and according to

> the ruler of the power of the air, the spirit that is now active in those who are disobedient.
> —*Ephesians 2:2 ISV*

If Satan the Devil can be called a *thĕ-ŏs,* then anyone else who is called *thĕ-ŏs* should not automatically be considered Yahweh's equal, as that term can be applied to different individuals among the heavenly beings. This means when Jesus is called *thĕ-ŏs* we must understand he is deserving of that title, but it does not imply he is equal to Yahweh. *Thĕ-ŏs* is used in the NT in a similar way as the Hebrew words *eloah* and *elohim* are used in the OT; just as all heavenly beings are called *eloah* (singular) or *elohim* (plural), so are they also called *thĕ-ŏs* (singular), or *thĕ-oi* (plural).

Chapter 4

One with God

At John 10:30 Jesus is quoted as saying, "I and the Father are one." ἐγὼ καὶ ὁ πατὴρ ἐσμεν ἕν (ĕgō kai hŏ patĕr esmen hen).

Many commentators understand the term *hen* (one) to indicate that Jesus was claiming to be God, which was the understanding of the Pharisees:

> The Jewish leaders replied, "We are not going to stone you for a good deed but for blasphemy, because you, a man, are claiming to be God."
> —*John 10:33: NET*

The Pharisees failed to understand most of what Jesus said, so their accusation is not surprising. To understand what Jesus meant, all we need to do is examine the immediate context, and then look at similar statements made by him and others.

> The Jewish leaders surrounded him and asked, "How long will you keep us in suspense? If you are the Christ, tell us plainly." Jesus replied, "I told you and you do not believe. The deeds I do in my Father's name testify about me. But you refuse to believe because *you are not my sheep. My sheep*

> *listen to my voice*, and *I know them*, and *they follow me*. I give them eternal life, and they will never perish; *no one will snatch them from my hand*. My Father, who has given them to me, is greater than all, *and no one can snatch them from my Father's hand. The Father and I are one." —John 10:24-30: NET (emphasis mine)*

The oneness is about protecting the sheep, not about Jesus being equal to the Father; no one can snatch them out of Jesus' hand, nor out of his Father's hand. Jesus made his intent clear by what he said in verse 29: "My Father, who has given them to me, is greater than all." Here Jesus admits his Father gave him the sheep (so at one time they were not his), and that his Father is "greater than all." There is no equality of being implied by these proclamations, only their united effort to protect the sheep.

> Note the safety of those who really belong to Christ. They are not only in his hand, but in the Father's, because the Father and He are one. "Your life is hid with Christ in God." Here is a double protection. They may wander far, lose joy and comfort, fall on dark and stormy times, but He is responsible for them, will seek them out, and bring them home. This also is true—that our relationship with Jesus involves our relationship with the Father. *Meyer, F.B, Through the Bible Day by Day, 1914, John 10:29.*

Being "one" with God or Christ does not make us their equal, just as it does not make Jesus equal to Yahweh, his Father. Being "one" unites us together in purpose. Note the following scriptures that proclaim oneness:

> But the one who joins himself to the Lord is one spirit with him. *—1 Corinthians 6:17 LEB*

> On that day you will know that I am in my Father, and you are in me, and I am in you. *—John 14:20 LEB*

> And I do not ask on behalf of these only, but also on behalf of those who believe in me through their word, that *they all may be one, just as you, Father, are in me and I am in you, that they also may be in us,* in order that the world may believe that you sent me. *And the glory that you have given to me, I have given to them, in order that they may be one, just as we are one— I in them, and you in me, in order that they may be completed in one,* so that the world may know that you sent me, and you have loved them just as you have loved me. *—John 17:20-23 LEB (emphasis mine)*

Faithful Christians will not become gods equal to Yahweh, but they will be united in purpose by their faithfulness to his will, just as Jesus was faithful.

> I [Jesus] am able to do nothing from myself. Just as I hear, I judge, and my judgment is just, because I do not seek my own will, but the will of the one who sent me. *—John 5:30 LEB*

After the Jewish leaders replied, "We are not going to stone you for a good deed but for blasphemy, because you, a man, are claiming to be God," Jesus replied:

> "Is it not written in your law, 'I said, you are gods?' If he called them 'gods' to whom the word of God came—and the scripture cannot be broken—do you say about he whom the Father set apart and sent into the world, 'You are blaspheming,' because I

> said, 'I am the Son of God?'" —*John 10:34-36 LEB* (Compare Psalm 82:6)

Claiming to be the "son" of God does not make one equal to God. Sons of any kind–human, animal, or spiritual–are alive because of their father.

> I [Jesus] live because of the Father. —*John 6:57 LEB*

The Pharisees drew the wrong conclusion, as do many of Christendom's theologians. Jesus plainly said:

> The Father is greater than I am. —*John 14:28 LEB*

Chapter 5

Clarifying the Name of God

William Shakespeare wrote: “A rose by any other name would smell as sweet,” implying that the names of things have no impact on their nature. While the nature of things may be independent from a name, a person's name is forever linked to their identity.

The human insistence on naming things is part of our created nature. We name our children, our pets, and other living beings. Why? Because each individual is unique and naming them sets them apart from everyone else. Some people name their possessions; cars, guitars, boats, and other things they deem of value in their lives. Why? The act of naming things elevates their importance. A person’s name becomes intertwined with their reputation. Say any famous person’s name and the reputation of the individual will come to mind. Our names define us in either a positive way or a negative way, based on our personal history.

A god by any other name obscures identity. In the Hebrew scriptures every god has a name. At least forty-nine individual gods, some with multiple names and variations in the spelling of their names. There were so many gentile gods that a name was essential to identify the god. A few gods were called Baal, but Baal just means *Lord*, so these gods had names like Baal Peor, Baal Berith, Baal Zephon, Baal Zebub, or Baal Hadad.

The Hebrew god had many titles but the Divine Name יהוה (yhwh) is his only proper name. The Divine Name יהוה (yhwh) is known as the Tetragrammaton (having four letters), and was probably pronounced as Yahweh, or something similar. In the OT, Yahweh is the most common term used to refer to the Almighty Creator (6,720 times in the LEB).

Because of a Hebrew superstition, יהוה (yhwh) stopped being pronounced when read aloud from scripture. The word אדנ (adohnai), *Lord*, was spoken to prevent speaking the Divine Name. This tradition eventually led to later copies of the Septuagint[3] having יהוה (yhwh) replaced with the Greek word κύριος (kyriŏs), *Lord*, or θεός (thĕ-ŏs), *God*.

> The papyrus containing fragments of Leviticus ii-v is written in a hand closely akin to that of Papyrus Fouad 266, characterized as already mentioned by the fact that the name of God is rendered by the Tetragrammaton in Hebrew square letters (יהוה), not by κύριος as later in the Christian MSS [manuscripts] of the Bible. *The Cairo Geniza, 1959 edition, pages 222, 224.*

Many English translations still follow this tradition by replacing יהוה (yhwh) with LORD or GOD, using capitals to distinguish them from Lord and God as translations for other Hebrew words.

In 1901 the *American Standard Version* was published and it restored the Divine Name to its original place in scripture with the anglicized spelling, Jehovah:

> The change first proposed in the Appendix—that which substitutes "Jehovah" for "Lord" and "God"

3. The earliest Greek translation of the OT, completed between 280 B.C.E. and 150 B.C.E.

> (printed in small capitals)—is one which will be unwelcome to many, because of the frequency and familiarity of the terms displaced. But the American Revisers, after a careful consideration, were brought to the unanimous conviction that a Jewish superstition, which regarded the Divine Name as too sacred to be uttered, ought no longer to dominate in the English or any other version of the Old Testament. . . This personal name, with its wealth of sacred associations, is now restored to the place in the sacred text to which it has an unquestionable claim. *American Revision Committee, 1901, American Standard Bible, Preface, Paragraph 8.*

Despite the efforts of the American Revision Committee, the tradition of replacing the Divine Name continues. When we see the words Lord and God in our English translations of the Bible, do we think of Yahweh or Jesus? Most modern English translations of the NT follow the Greek text and continue to use Lord or God in quotations from the OT. This continues to hide the name of the Creator. Context should guide us. When we read a quotation in the NT from the OT that refers to Yahweh, who should we think about? Who did the Hebrew prophets have in mind?

Why do some Christian theologians continue to hide God's proper name? His reputation is tied to his name, which is why he said:

> I am Yahweh; that is my name, and I do not give my glory to another, nor my praise to the idols. *—Isaiah 42:8 LEB*

Yahweh recognizes the importance of names:

> And I will make you a great nation, and I will bless you, and I will make your name great. And you will be a blessing. *Genesis —12:2 LEB*

> Your name shall no longer be called Abram, but your name shall be Abraham, for I will make you the father of a multitude of nations. —*Genesis 17:5 LEB*

> But now thus says Yahweh, he who created you, Jacob, and he who formed you, Israel: "You must not fear, for I have redeemed you. I have called you by your name; you are mine." —*Isaiah 43:1 LEB*

> And I will give you the treasures of darkness and treasures of secret places so that you may know that I am Yahweh, the one who calls you by your name, the God of Israel, for the sake of my servant Jacob, and Israel my chosen one. And I call you by your name; I give you a name of honor, though you do not know me. —*Isaiah 45:3 LEB*

Since Yahweh honors the names of those who honor him, why do most Christians today not honor his name by using it? Not using a person's name dishonors them. I have heard many theologians refer to Yahweh as "Father God," "El Shaddai" (God Almighty), "Lord God," "Creator," and other titles that identify his characteristics, but never, "Yahweh," the name bound to his reputation. This is the same as calling someone "Man" or "Woman" while refusing to use their proper name. Would we not find this insulting if done to us?

Jesus taught his followers to pray: "When you pray, say: 'Father, may your name be honored; may your kingdom come.'" (Luke 11:2 NET)

How can we honor God's name if we refuse to use it?

An interesting prophecy by Jesus relates to his name:

> Not everyone who says to me, "Lord, Lord," will enter into the kingdom of heaven. —*Matthew 7:21 LEB*

He tells those people who profess to be his disciples:

> I never knew you. Depart from me, you who practice lawlessness! *—Matthew 7:23 LEB*

We cannot truly know someone if we don't know their name. Calling Yahweh, "God," or "Lord," puts him on the same level with all the Baal (Lord) gods who were the center of Israel's apostate worship. If we use Jesus' name, then should we not also use Yahweh's name? If we refuse to use Yahweh's name, why should he take note of our names?

James says, "Draw near to God, and he will draw near to you," (James 4:8 LEB). This is in harmony with 2 Chronicles 15:2: "Yahweh is with you while you are with him. And if you will seek him he will be found by you. But if you forsake him he will forsake you." (LEB). By refusing to use Yahweh's name, we are forsaking him, and he can rightfully say to us, "I never knew you."

Hebrews 7:25 says, "Therefore also he [Jesus] is able to save completely those who draw near to God [Yahweh] through him, because he always lives in order to intercede on their behalf."(LEB - See 1 Timothy 2:5)

So the questions must be asked: "Who has ascended to heaven, and then descended? Who has collected the wind in his hands? Who has wrapped up waters in a garment? Who has established all the farthest points of the earth? What is his name, and what is his son's name? Surely you know!" *—Proverbs 30:4 ISV*

God's Name Replaced

The following scriptures are a small sample to show the removal of the Divine Name in the Greek New Testament.

Isaiah 40:3-5 LEB

A voice is calling in the wilderness, "Clear the way of Yahweh! . . . And the glory of Yahweh shall be revealed, and all humankind together shall see it, for the mouth of Yahweh has spoken."

> For this is the one who was spoken about by the prophet Isaiah, saying, "The voice of one crying out in the wilderness, 'Prepare the way of the Lord, make his paths straight.'" —*Matthew 3:3 LEB*

> As it is written in the book of the words of the prophet Isaiah, "The voice of one crying out in the wilderness, 'Prepare the way of the Lord, make his paths straight! . . . and all flesh will see the salvation of God.'" —*Luke 3:4-6 LEB*

> He [John the Baptist] said, "I am 'the voice of one crying out in the wilderness, 'Make straight the way of the Lord,'" just as Isaiah the prophet said." —*John 1:23 LEB*

Deuteronomy 8:3 LEB

. . . in order to make you know that not by bread alone but by all that goes out of the mouth of Yahweh humankind shall live.

> It is written, "Man will not live on bread alone, but on every word that comes out of the mouth of God."—*Matthew 4:4 LEB*

> And Jesus replied to him, "It is written, 'Man will not live on bread alone.'" —*Luke 4:4 LEB*

Deuteronomy 6:16 LEB

You shall not put Yahweh your God to the test, as you tested him at Massah.

> Jesus said to him, "On the other hand it is written, 'You are not to put the Lord your God to the test.'" —*Matthew 4:7 LEB*

Joel 2:32 LEB

And it will happen—everyone who calls on the name of Yahweh will be rescued, because on Mount Zion and in Jerusalem there will be those who escape, as Yahweh said, and among the survivors whom Yahweh is calling.

> "And it will be that everyone who calls upon the name of the Lord will be saved." —*Acts 2:21 LEB*

> For "everyone who calls upon the name of the Lord will be saved." —*Romans 10:13 LEB*

Psalm 2:7 LEB

I will tell the decree; Yahweh said to me: "You are my son; today I have begotten you."

> For to which of the angels did he ever say, "You are my son, today I have begotten you." —*Hebrews 1:5 LEB*

Chapter 6

The Image of God

The designation, "Image of God," has been interpreted different ways. How did the original authors of the Bible intend this term to be understood?

> IMAGE OF GOD A phrase found several times in the book of Genesis (Gen 1:7–27; 5:1–3; 9:6). Distinguishes humankind from the animal and plant kingdoms. Elevates humankind above all terrestrial created things so as to exercise benevolent and ethical stewardship over creation. Image of God language is found in the New Testament as part of the Christian's responsibility to imitate Christ, who is the image(r) of God par excellence. *Heiser, Michael S., Editor 2016, Image of God,* The *Lexham Bible Dictionary, Logos Bible Software, Faithlife, LLC.*

The phrase refers to traits given to humans by God to fulfill our created purpose. Humans were created to be a reflection of God on Earth; to be God's representatives. The *elohim* who reside in the spirit realm also share these traits since they are called "Sons of God," as Adam is called a Son of God. (See Job 38:7; Luke 3:38)

In Genesis, Yahweh is speaking to more than one individual regarding the creation of humankind.

> And God said, "Let us make humankind in our image and according to our likeness . . ." —*Genesis 1:26 LEB*

Other statements in Genesis are also in the plural:

> And Yahweh God said, "Look—the man has become as one of us, to know good and evil." —*Genesis 3:22 LEB*

> Come, let us go down and confuse their language there, so that they will not understand each other's language. —*Genesis 11:7 LEB*

In these verses Yahweh is speaking to the heavenly Sons of God. This is more obvious in *1 Kings 22*, where the prophet Micaiah reveals a gathering in heaven where Yahweh asks the Sons of God what to do about Ahab:

> And he [Micaiah] said, "Therefore, hear the word of Yahweh. I saw Yahweh sitting on his throne with all the hosts of heaven standing beside him from his right hand and from his left hand. And Yahweh said, 'Who will entice Ahab so that he will go up and fall at Ramoth-Gilead?' . . . Then a spirit came out and stood before Yahweh and said, 'I will entice him,' and Yahweh said to him, 'How?' He said, 'I will go out and I will be a false spirit in the mouth of all his prophets.' And he [Yahweh] said, 'You shall entice and succeed, go out and do so.' So then, see that Yahweh has placed a false spirit in the mouth of all of these your prophets, and Yahweh has

> spoken disaster concerning you." *1 Kings 22:19-23 —WEB* (See Understanding Spirit)

The incident related by Micaiah, and the plural statements in Genesis, reveals to us that Yahweh includes the Sons of God in his decision making and actions; he asks for their suggestions, as a good father would ask for feedback from his children when making major decisions. He does this because they are made in his image; they reflect his qualities—they were created with the ability to analyze and form opinions, not exist as mindless creatures of instinct.

Returning to Genesis 1:26: Please note that both male and female humans are made in the image of God. So being an "image of God" cannot refer to gender, but must refer to traits instilled in us by God.

> It is best to take the term as referring to the whole dignity of man, in virtue of his fundamental affinity to God. It implies the possession by man of a free, self-conscious, rational and moral personality, like unto that of God—a nature capable of distinguishing right and wrong, of choosing the right and rejecting the wrong, and of ascending to the heights of spiritual attainment and communion with God. This involves a separation of man from the beast, and his supremacy as the culmination of the creative process. *Orr, James, Editor, 1929, ISBE, 1980 Edition, Eerdmans Publishing Company, Vol. 3, pg.1450, Image: Man as Made in the Divine Image.*

This aspect of being an "Image of God" applies to Jesus as it does to all sons of God. A person who is an image of someone reflects their attributes, and Jesus is the perfect reflection of Yahweh. This quality does not make Jesus equal to the Father, because Yahweh, the Almighty God, is unique; all created beings are subservient to Yahweh and Jesus is a created being.

> He [Jesus] is the image of the invisible God, the firstborn of all creation. —*Colossians 1:15 ESV*

> Jesus told them, "Truly, I tell all of you with certainty, the Son can do nothing on his own accord, but only what he sees the Father doing. What the Father does, the Son does likewise." —*John 5:19 ISV*

> You heard me [Jesus] say to you, "I am going away and I am coming back to you." If you loved me, you would be glad that I am going to the Father, because the Father is greater than I am. —*John 14:28 NET*

> Jesus said to her, "Do not cling to me, for I have not yet ascended to the Father; but go to my brothers and say to them, 'I am ascending to my Father and your Father, to my God and your God.'" —*John 20:17 ESV*

As the image of God "par excellence," Jesus represents the standard for all Christians to follow.

> And we know that all things work together for good for those who love God, who are called according to his purpose, because those whom he foreknew *he also predestined to be conformed to the image of his Son, that his Son would be the firstborn among many brothers and sisters. —Romans 8:28, 29 NET (emphasis mine)*

> I am coming soon. Hold on to what you have so that no one can take away your crown. The one who conquers *I will make a pillar in the temple of my God,*

> and he will never depart from it. *I will write on him the name of my God* and *the name of the city of my God* (the new Jerusalem that comes down out of heaven from my God), *and my new name* as well. — *Revelation 3:11,12 NET (emphasis mine)*

Just as the term, "Sons of God," is used to identify all created beings in the spiritual realm, (see Job 38:7), the term "Image of God" is used to identify all beings created with attributes that reflect the Creator. Because of free will, how well they demonstrate those qualities is up to them.

Chapter 7

The Characteristics of God

Without Beginning or End

> Before the mountains were born and you brought forth the earth and the world, even from everlasting to everlasting, you are God. —*Psalm 90:2 LEB*
>
> Your throne is established from of old; you are from everlasting. —*Psalm 93:2 LEB*
>
> Behold, God is great, beyond our knowledge; the number of His years is unsearchable. —*Job 36:26 JPS*
>
> But Yahweh is the true God, he is the living God, and an everlasting king. —*Jeremiah 10:10 LEB*

Yahweh has always existed and will always exist. His name means *the existing one*. He did not come to be as a result of universal processes. He created the universe.

Cannot Be Seen with Human Eyes

No man hath seen God at any time; the only begotten Son, who is in the bosom of the Father, he hath declared him. *—John 1:18 ASV*

But he said, "You are not able to see my face, because a human will not see me and live."
—Exodus 33:20 LEB

Now to the King of the ages, immortal, invisible, to the only God, be honor and glory forever and ever. Amen. *—1 Timothy 1:17 LEB*

Outstanding Qualities

The Rock, his work is perfect, for all his ways are just; he is a faithful God, and without injustice; righteous and upright is he. *—Deuteronomy 32:4 LEB*

Look up at the sky! Who created the stars you see? The one who leads them out like an army, he knows how many there are and calls each one by name! His power is so great—not one of them is ever missing! —*Isaiah 40:26 GNB*

And Yahweh passed over before him, and he proclaimed, "Yahweh, Yahweh, God, who is compassionate and gracious, slow to anger, and abounding with loyal love and faithfulness."
—Exodus 34:6 LEB

With him are wisdom and powerful deeds, and to him belong counsel and understanding. *Job 12:13 LEB*

For you, O Lord, are good and forgiving, and abundant in loyal love for all who call to you. *—Psalm 86:5 LEB*

And what if God, wanting to demonstrate his wrath and to make known his power, endured with much patience vessels of wrath prepared for destruction? And he did so in order that he could make known the riches of his glory upon vessels of mercy that he prepared beforehand for glory, us whom he also called, not only from the Jews but also from the Gentiles? As he also says in Hosea, "I will call those who were not my people, 'My people,' and those who were not loved, 'Loved.' And it will be in the place where it was said to them, 'You are not my people,' there they will be called 'sons of the living God.'" *—Romans 9:22-26 LEB*

Now if any of you lacks wisdom, let him ask for it from God, who gives to all without reservation and not reproaching, and it will be given to him. *—James 1:5 LEB*

Behold, we consider blessed those who have endured. You have heard about the patient endurance of Job, and you saw the outcome from the Lord, that the Lord is compassionate and merciful. *—James 5:11 LEB*

The Lord is not delaying the promise, as some consider slowness, but is being patient toward you, because he does not want any to perish, but all to come to repentance. *—2 Peter 3:9 LEB*

Yahweh has comforted his people, and he will take pity on his afflicted ones. *—Isaiah 49:13 LEB*

Do you know about the hovering of the clouds, the marvelous works of the one with perfect knowledge? *—Job 37:16 LEB*

Have you not known, or have you not heard? Yahweh is the God of eternity, the creator of the ends of the earth! He is not faint, and he does not grow weary! There is no searching his understanding. —*Isaiah 40:28 LEB*

Go, and proclaim these words toward the north, and say, "Return, apostate Israel," declares Yahweh. "I will not cause my anger to fall on you. For I am loyal," declares Yahweh. "I will not be angry forever." *—Jeremiah 3:12 LEB*

For I, Yahweh, have not changed, and you, O children of Jacob, have not perished. *—Malachi 3:6 LEB*

For God is not a God of disorder but of peace. *—1 Corinthians 14:33 LEB*

In order that through two unchangeable things, in which it is impossible for God to lie, we who have taken refuge may have powerful encouragement to hold fast to the hope set before us. *—Hebrews 6:18 LEB*

And the four living creatures, each one of them, had six wings apiece, full of eyes around and inside, and they do not have rest day and night, saying, "Holy, holy, holy is the Lord God All-Powerful, the one who was and the one who is and the one who is coming!" *—Revelation 4:8 LEB*

Now the Lord is the Spirit, and where the Spirit of the Lord is, there is freedom. —*2 Corinthians 3:17 LEB*

Claiming to be wise, they became fools, and exchanged the glory of the immortal God with the likeness of an image of mortal human beings and birds and quadrupeds and reptiles. —*Romans 1:23 LEB*

For the eyes of Yahweh roam throughout all the earth to strengthen those whose heart is fully devoted to him. —*2 Chronicles 16:9 LEB*

For the eyes of the Lord are on the righteous, and his ears are open to their prayer. But the face of the Lord is against those who do evil. —*1 Peter 3:13 LEB*

Will the one who planted the ear not hear? Will the one who formed the eye not see? —*Psalm 94.9 LEB*

Woe to the one who strives with his maker, a potsherd among potsherds of earth! Does the clay say to the one who fashions it, "What are you making?" and "Your work has no hands"? —*Isaiah 45:9 LEB*

In every place, the eyes of Yahweh keep watch over the evil and the good. —*Proverbs 15:3 LEB*

And no creature is hidden in the sight of him, but all things are naked and laid bare to the eyes of him to whom we must give our account. —*Hebrews 4:13 LEB*

For my eyes are on all their ways, they are not hidden from before me, and their iniquity is not concealed from before my eyes. *—Jeremiah 16:17 LEB*

Not Omnipresent but In a Specific Place

You [Yahweh] must listen to the plea of your servant and your people Israel which they pray toward this place; and you must hear from the place where you live, from heaven you must hear and you must forgive. *—1 Kings 8:30 LEB*

For Christ did not enter into a sanctuary made by hands, a mere copy of the true one, but into heaven itself, now to appear in the presence of God on our behalf. *—Hebrews 9:24 LEB*

And do not call anyone your father on earth, for one is your heavenly Father. . . and the one who swears by heaven swears by the throne of God and by the one who sits on it. *—Matthew 23:9,22 LEB*

Yahweh is in his holy temple; Yahweh is in the heavens on his throne. *—Psalm 11:4 LEB*

If they dig into Sheol, from there my hand will take them, and even if they climb up to heaven, from there I will bring them down. *—Amos 9:2 LEB*

"For my thoughts are not your thoughts, and your ways are not my ways," declares Yahweh. "For as the heavens are higher than the earth, so my ways are higher than your ways, and my thoughts than your thoughts. For just as the rain and the snow come down from heaven, and they do not return there except they have watered the earth thoroughly and cause it to bring forth and sprout, and give seed to the sower and bread to the eater, so shall be my word that goes out from my mouth. It shall not return to me without success, but shall accomplish what I desire and be successful in the thing for which I sent it." —*Isaiah 55:8-11 LEB*

The God of Jews and Gentiles

Or is God the God of the Jews only? Is he not also the God of the Gentiles? Yes, also of the Gentiles. —*Romans 3:29 LEB*

So Peter opened his mouth and said, "In truth I understand that God is not one who shows partiality, but in every nation the one who fears him and who does what is right is acceptable to him." —*Acts 10:34,35 LEB*

And when they heard these things, they became silent and praised God, saying, "Then God has granted the repentance leading to life to the Gentiles also!" —*Acts 11:18 LEB*

For your husband is your maker, his name is Yahweh of hosts; and your redeemer is the holy one of Israel, he is called the God of all of the earth. —*Isaiah 54:5 LEB*

Chapter 8

The Justice of God

> Thus has Yahweh of Armies spoken, saying, "Execute true judgment, and show kindness and compassion every man to his brother. Don't oppress the widow, nor the fatherless, the foreigner, nor the poor; and let none of you devise evil against his brother in your heart." *—Zechariah 7:9,10 WEB*

Yahweh's defining qualities are love, wisdom, power, and justice. Each of these characteristics defines his personality: His love is revealed in his wisdom, justice, and power. His wisdom is a result of his love, justice, and power. His power is held in check by his wisdom, love and justice. His justice is determined by his love, wisdom and power. He never asks his creation to do something he himself would not do.

> No one who is being tempted should say, "I am being tempted by God," for God cannot be tempted by evil, and he himself tempts no one. *—James 1:13 LEB*

To understand God's justice, we must understand sin. Sin is lawlessness (See 1 John 3:4). Lawlessness is uncontrolled or unregulated conduct. Lawlessness in the Bible is conduct contrary to Yahweh's intended purpose for his creation. It embodies everything opposed to Yahweh's holy nature.

> I prayed to Yahweh my God, and made confession, and said, "Oh, Lord, the great and dreadful God, who keeps covenant and loving kindness with those who love him and keep his commandments, we have sinned, and have dealt perversely, and have done wickedly, and have rebelled, even turning aside from your precepts and from your ordinances. —*Daniel 9:4, 5 WEB*

Yahweh's love demands that lawlessness must be eliminated for the peaceful future of His children.

> Do not fret because of evildoers; do not be envious of doers of wickedness. For like the grass they will dry up quickly, and like the green vegetation they will wither. Trust Yahweh and do good. . . . For evildoers will be cut off, but those who wait for Yahweh will possess the land. And yet a little while and the wicked will not be, and you will look carefully upon his place, but he will not be. —*Psalm 37:1-3,9,10 WEB*

> When the wicked flourish like grass and all the workers of evil blossom, it is so they can be destroyed forever. —*Psalm 92:7 LEB*

> Wait for Yahweh and keep his way, and he will exalt you to possess the land. When the wicked are cut-off, you will see it. I have seen the wicked acting violently and spreading himself out like a luxuriant native tree. Then he passed on and behold, he was not. And I sought him, but he could not be found. Observe the blameless and look at the upright, for

> there is a future for a man of peace. But transgressors shall be destroyed altogether. The future of the wicked shall be cut off. —*Psalm 37: 34-38 LEB*

Our standing with God is determined by his justice. All of Adam's descendants are born into lawlessness. Therefore, without redemption our futures are limited.

> There is no one righteous, not even one . . . for all have sinned and fall short of the glory of God. —*Romans 3:10, 23 LEB.*

> For the wages of sin is death. —*Romans 6:23 ESV*

Death is the punishment for sin. This is the legal standing established by Yahweh when he told Adam, "From every tree of the garden you may freely eat, but from the tree of the knowledge of good and evil you shall not eat, for in the day that you eat from it you shall surely die," (Genesis 2:16,17 LEB). By rejecting Yahweh's authority, Adam fell into lawlessness and received the punishment of death.

Please note, this punishment was not eternal torture in a fiery hell. It was an eternal loss of life, for Yahweh told Adam, "By the sweat of your brow you shall eat bread, until your return to the ground. For from it you were taken; for you are dust, and to dust you shall return," (Genesis 3:19 LEB).

Adam knowingly rejected Yahweh's authority. His offspring did not. We were all born into a lawless world, we did not choose it. Because of this, Yahweh's love demanded a solution for Adam's offspring that would be legally acceptable, not only by Him, but by all heavenly beings who witnessed Adam's fall from grace. The solution was the Messiah, the seed of the woman who would one day strike the head of the serpent (see Genesis 3:15). This seed was Jesus, born a perfect man equal to Adam.

> For just as in Adam all die, so also in Christ all will be made alive. . . Thus, also it is written, "The first man, Adam, became a living soul"; the last Adam became a life-giving spirit. *—1 Corinthians 15:22, 45 LEB*

By willfully sacrificing his perfect human life, Jesus paid the legal price for the lives of Adam's offspring.

> He bought you for a price. So, use your bodies for God's glory. *—1 Corinthians 6:20 GNB*

This undeserved kindness from Yahweh, to send his son to give up his life for Adam's lawless offspring, is the ultimate demonstration of his love (see John 3:16), and satisfies his perfect justice.

> I have complete confidence in the gospel; it is God's power to save all who believe, first the Jews and also the Gentiles. For the gospel reveals how God puts people right with himself: it is through faith from beginning to end. As the scripture says, "The person who is put right with God through faith shall live." *—Romans 1:16-17 GNB*

The punishment for sin is death (see Romans 6:23). Yahweh does not torture the wicked eternally. Sane people recognize that torture is evil, that's why it is banned in nations with a strong moral foundation. This quality of moral uprightness comes to us from Yahweh; we were created in His image. Torture is evil and God is not tempted by evil (See James 1:13).

The prophetic statements in Scripture about throwing the wicked into fire, or placing them in eternal torment, are metaphors for complete destruction and punishment that once executed has everlasting effects.

Gehenna, the Greek name for the Valley of Hinnom, the deep, narrow valley on the south and southwest side of Jerusalem, once a place for Baal and Moloch worship, was used in the first-century C.E. as a garbage dump. Bodies of dead animals and criminals were placed there to burn. Both Jesus and James used Gehenna as a symbolic destination for those condemned by God, like the Lake of Fire in John's Revelation. The effects of fire are everlasting; once something is burned, it is gone forever. (See original Greek versions of Matthew 5:22, 29,30; 10:28; 18:9; 25:15; 23:55; Mark 9:43, 45; Luke:12:5; James 3:6. See also WEB, WNT and YLT where γέεννα is rendered *Gehenna,* while often rendered *hell* in other translations.)

> The Valley of Hinnom near Jerusalem where Solomon built "an high place" for Moloch . . . Because some of the Israelites . . . sacrificed their children to Moloch there, the valley came to be regarded as a place of abomination. In a later period it was made a place for the dumping of refuse, and perpetual fires were maintained to prevent pestilence.—*The New Funk & Wagnalls Encyclopedia, 1950, Volume 15, page 5576.*

> GEHENNA . . . It became the common lay-stall of the city, where the dead bodies of criminals, and the carcasses of animals, and every other kind of filth was cast. — *Smith's Dictionary of the Bible, 1889, Volume 1, page 879.*

Another example of burning as punishment that has everlasting effects, is the prophecy about the destruction of Edom:

> The rivers of Edom will turn into tar, and the soil will turn into sulfur. The whole country will burn like tar. It will burn day and night, and smoke will rise from it forever. The land will lie waste age after age,

> and no one will ever travel through it again. —*Isaiah 34:9,10 GNB*

We know from observation that the smoke is not rising today and the country is not burning day and night. We know from the very next verse that "owls and ravens" will take over the land, indicating it will still be habitable. (Isaiah 34:11). The intent of this prophecy is revealed in verse 12:

> There will be no king to rule the country, and the leaders will all be gone. —*Isaiah 34:12 GNB*

The nation of Edom was completely destroyed. There are no Edomites living today. The nation was metaphorically burned up.

Destruction as the ultimate end of the wicked was foretold by the Apostle Paul:

> And to you who are being afflicted, rest with us at the revelation of the Lord Jesus from heaven with his powerful angels, with burning flame giving punishment to those who do not know God and who do not obey the gospel of our Lord Jesus, who will pay the penalty of *eternal destruction,* away from the presence of the Lord and from the glory of his strength. —*2 Thessalonians 1: 7-9 LEB (emphasis mine)*

The word translated "destruction" in 2 Thessalonians 1:9 is ὄλεθρος, *ŏl-eth-rŏs*, from the root ὄλλυμι, *ŏllumi,* (to destroy), and means ruin, death, destruction.

There is no greater punishment than permanent loss of life; the legal result of rejecting Yahweh's authority. (Compare Genesis 2:17)

At Revelation 20:14,15 we read: "And Death and Hades were thrown into the lake of fire. This is the second death—the lake of fire. And if anyone was not found written in the book of life, he was thrown into the lake of fire," (LEB).

Death is a condition, which is thrown into the lake of fire. Hades (rendered Hell in KJV) refers to the grave, the abode of the dead. Both Death and Hades suffer the *second death* in the lake of fire. In other words, both Death and Hades are burned up, completely destroyed, along with everyone not written in the book of life.

> . . . and death will not exist any longer. —*Revelation 21: 4 LEB*

The second death is a death with no possible resurrection. This implies permanent loss of existence.

The death all humans experience due to Adam, was viewed by Jesus to be like sleep; an unconscious state from which we can be revived.

> . . . this he [Jesus] said to them, "Our friend Lazarus has fallen asleep, but I am going so that I can awaken him." So the disciples said to him, "Lord, if he has fallen asleep, he will get well." (Now Jesus had been speaking about his death, but they thought that he was speaking about real sleep.) So Jesus then said to them plainly, "Lazarus has died." —*John 11:11-14 LEB*

Lazarus was not the only person to be resurrected by Jesus:

> And as he [Jesus] approached the gate of the town, behold, a man who had died was being carried out, his mother's only son, and she was a widow. And a large crowd from the town was with her. And when the Lord saw her, he had compassion for her and said to her, "Do not weep!" And he came up and touched the bier, and those who were carrying it stopped. And he said, "Young man, I say to you, get

> up!" And the dead man sat up and began to speak, and he gave him to his mother. *—Luke 7:14,15 LEB*

> While he was still speaking, someone came from the synagogue ruler's house, saying, "Your daughter is dead! Trouble the Teacher no longer!" . . . But Jesus, when he heard this, replied to him, "Do not be afraid! Only believe, and she will be healed." . . . he took her hand and called, saying, "Child, get up." And her spirit returned, and she got up immediately, and he ordered something to be given to her to eat.— *Luke 8-49-55 LEB*

Resurrection is guaranteed for both the righteous and the unrighteous.

> Therefore, having overlooked the times of ignorance, God now commands all people everywhere to repent, because he has set a day on which he is going to judge the world in righteousness by a man he has appointed. He has provided assurance of this to everyone by raising this man [Jesus] from the dead. *—Acts:17:31 LEB*

> But now Christ has been raised from the dead, the first fruits of those who have fallen asleep. For since through a man came death, also through a man came the resurrection of the dead. For just as in Adam all die, so also in Christ all will be made alive. —1 Corinthians 15:20-22

While both the righteous and the unrighteous will have a resurrection (see Acts 24:15), at the final judgment all those who persist in lawlessness will suffer the *second death*—eternal loss of life.

It is a loving thing for Yahweh to remove the wicked from his creation. If he did not, where would His love be for those who love him? He has demonstrated much patience by tolerating the wicked since Adam's fall. The reason is simple:

> The Lord is not delaying the promise, as some consider slowness, but is being patient toward you, because he does not want any to perish, but all to come to repentance. *—2 Peter 3:9 LEB*

The Need for Justice

When Satan replied to Eve in the Garden, he slandered Yahweh. He implied Yahweh was keeping things of benefit from Adam and Eve; He said Yahweh had lied.

> Now the serpent was more subtle than any animal of the field which Yahweh God had made. He said to the woman, "Has God really said, 'You shall not eat of any tree of the garden?'"
> The woman said to the serpent, "We may eat fruit from the trees of the garden, but not the fruit of the tree which is in the middle of the garden. God has said, 'You shall not eat of it. You shall not touch it, lest you die.'"
> The serpent said to the woman, "You won't really die, for God knows that in the day you eat it, your eyes will be opened, and you will be like God, knowing good and evil." *—Genesis 3:1-5 WEB*

In the book of Job, Satan claims men only serve Yahweh for the benefits he provides.

> Then Satan answered Yahweh, and said, "Does Job fear God for nothing? Haven't you made a hedge around him, and around his house, and around all

> that he has, on every side? You have blessed the work of his hands, and his substance is increased in the land. But stretch out your hand now, and touch all that he has, and he will renounce you to your face." *—Job 1:9-11 WEB*

Job proved faithful to Yahweh, so Satan returned and said:

> "Skin for skin. Yes, all that a man has he will give for his life. But stretch out your hand now, and touch his bone and his flesh, and he will renounce you to your face." *—Job 2: 4-5 WEB*

These accounts in Genesis and Job reveal the continuing slander of Yahweh by Satan. Slander is a direct assault on a person's reputation. Eliminating Satan for his actions would be easy for Yahweh, but the questions regarding his reputation would remain among all the other spirit beings who knew about Satan's allegations. Yahweh's wisdom and sense of justice held his power in check. Yahweh allowed Satan to continue, knowing that over time His reputation will be restored once all of Satan's allegations are proven to be lies.

> "I will sanctify my great name, which has been profaned among the nations, which you have profaned among them. Then the nations will know that I am Yahweh," says the Lord Yahweh, "when I am proven holy in you before their eyes. *—Ezekiel 36:23 WEB*

> "I will magnify myself, and sanctify myself, and I will make myself known in the eyes of many nations. Then they will know that I am Yahweh."*—Ezekiel 38:23 WEB*

> I will make my holy name known among my people

> Israel. I won't allow my holy name to be profaned any more. Then the nations will know that I am Yahweh, the Holy One in Israel. Behold, it comes, and it will be done," says the Lord Yahweh.—*Ezekiel 39:7,8 WEB*

Free Will, Free Choice

The fall of Adam and Eve was always a possibility. The rebellion of Satan was always a possibility. The failure of the Sons of God to rule justly over the nations was always a possibility (see Understanding Spirit/Greek Spirit #6). They were all given free will to choose and they chose wrong.

The possibility of failing is what makes integrity powerful. When asked to sacrifice his son, Abraham never flinched. Yahweh's response is enlightening:

> Then he [Abraham] picked up the knife to kill him.
> But the angel of the LORD called to him from heaven, "Abraham, Abraham!"
> He answered, "Yes, here I am."
> "Don't hurt the boy or do anything to him," he said. "*Now I know* that you honor and obey God, because you have not kept back your only son."
> *—Genesis 22:10-12 GNB (emphasis mine)*

With free will, our choices are not known until they are made; even Yahweh can be surprised. He prefers a creation that demonstrates integrity by choice, not out of intimidation, or programmed instinct.

Chapter 9

Understanding Spirit

Spirit is another word that has multiple meanings in English, Hebrew, and Greek.

The English word is derived from the Latin *spiritus* "breath," which comes from the Latin *spirare* "breathe."

The definitions of the English *spirit* are many:

1. Life force of a person: the vital force that keeps a human being alive.
2. Will or sense of self: He retained an indomitable spirit.
3. Mental Attitude:
   a. Enthusiasm and energy: He responded with spirit.
   b. Kindness: She has a generous spirit.
   c. State of mind: The spirit of compromise.
4. Group loyalty: the enthusiasm and loyalty through belonging to a group; Team spirit.
5. Important influence: somebody or something that is a divine, inspiring, or animating influence.
6. Real meaning: the intention behind something such as a law or decree, rather than its literal interpretation.

7. Shared outlook: the prevailing mood characteristic of a place or time: The spirit of 1776.
8. Person: someone who displays a particular quality; He was a jovial spirit
9. Soul: in some beliefs, a non-material, supernatural being that either leaves the physical body after death, or who's origin is in the supernatural realm, e.g. a ghost, angel, or demon.
10. Alcoholic drink: a strong alcoholic liquor made by distillation (often used in the plural); He never drank spirits.

Because of the many ways the word *spirit* is used in English, our comprehension of the intended use in the Bible can be difficult even when the context is understood. To ensure accurate comprehension, it is necessary to know how the word was understood by those who wrote the scriptures.

Hebrew Spirit

The Hebrew terms of importance are נשמה, *nesh-aw-maw*, and רוּח, *roo'-ahkh*. These words differ slightly in meaning, both signifying primarily "wind," then "breath," though the former suggests a gentler blowing, the latter often a blast. As applied to persons there is no clear distinction between the words. Yet of the two *nesh-aw-maw* is preferred to describe the physiological breath, and is used less frequently than *roo'-ahkh,* which is translated often as *spirit,* as well as *breath* and *wind.* (See ISBE, 1980 edition, Volume 1, page 518.)

1. Spirit as Supernatural Influence

> . . . and the spirit *(roo'-ahkh)* of God hovered over the face of the waters. —*Genesis 1:2 JPS*

This *spirit* identifies the means by which Yahweh accomplished his creation—the force behind Yahweh's activity; how he achieves his purpose.

> You [Yahweh] send forth your Spirit *(roo'-ahkh)*, they are created, and you renew the face of the ground. —*Psalm 104: 30 LEB*

This scripture identifies the "tool" Yahweh uses to accomplish his creative tasks. A human craftsman would use the force of his hands and fingers to produce things. Yahweh uses the force of his spirit, which has been called his "hands" and "fingers." (See Psalm 8:3; 19:1.)

2. Spirit as Breath: the Principle of Life

> For as long as my breath *(nesh-aw-maw)* is in me, and the spirit *(roo'-ahkh)* of God is in my nose, my lips surely will not speak falseness. —*Job 27:3,4 LEB*

> The "spirit of God" here means the breath that God breathed into man when he created him, Gen 2:7. It would seem probable that there was an allusion to that fact by the language here, and that the knowledge of the way in which man was created was thus handed down by tradition. *Burnes, Albert, Notes on the Bible, 1847-1885, Job 27:3.*

Every animal on Earth needs to breathe to live. Once that is taken from us the result is the same; we return to the dust.

> For what happens to the children of man and what happens to the beasts is the same; as one dies, so dies the other. They all have the same breath *(roo'-ahkh)*, and man has no advantage over the beasts, for all is vanity. All go unto one place; all are of the dust, and all return to dust. —*Ecclesiastes 3:19,20 JPS* (Compare Psalm 104:29)

3. Spirit as the Inner Life (Heart)

> "Like a city broken down and without a wall, so is he whose spirit *(roo'-ahkh)* is without restraint." —*Proverbs 25:28 JPS*

The force of human nature, what drives us all, is our individual desires. If we are in control of our desires we have a better chance of succeeding. If we are out of control the odds increase for failure. (Compare 1 Timothy 6:10; 1 Peter 4:3-5).

4. Spirit Sons of God (Heavenly Beings)

> I saw Yahweh sitting on his throne with all the hosts of heaven standing beside him from his right hand and from his left hand. . . . Then a spirit *(roo'-ahkh)* came out and stood before Yahweh. —*1 Kings 22:19, 21 LEB*

> And the Spirit *(roo'-ahkh)* lifted me up, and I heard behind me the sound of a great earthquake when the glory of Yahweh rose from its place. . . . And the Spirit *(roo'-ahkh)* lifted me and took me, and I went in

> bitterness in the heat of my spirit *(roo'-ahkh)*, and the hand of Yahweh was strong on me. *—Ezekiel 3:12, 14 LEB*

Greek Spirit

The Greek word translated *spirit* is πνεῦμα, *p-nĕü-mah*, from the root πνέω, *p-nĕ-ōh* (I breathe), and has as its earliest meanings *breath* and *wind*. The English word *pneumatic* comes from the Greek πνευματικός, *p-nĕu-mahti-kŏs* (the characteristics [business] of breathing or manipulating air).

1. Spirit as Wind: A Forceful Breeze

> "The wind (*p-nĕü-mah*) blows wherever it wishes, and you hear the sound of it, but you do not know where it comes from and where it is going. So is everyone who is born of the Spirit (*p-nĕú-mah*)."
> *—John 3:8 LEB*

Like the wind, Yahweh's spirit is invisible, but it is a force that affects the real world, and can change our course in life and steer us down a path not previously considered ("So is everyone who is born of the Spirit"). This is in harmony with the use of *spirit* as noted above under Hebrew Spirit #1.

2. Spirit as Breath: The Principle of Life

Compare these three translations of Matthew 27:50:

> And Jesus cried out again with a loud voice and gave up his spirit *(p-nĕü-mah)*. *—LEB*

> Jesus again gave a loud cry and breathed *(p-nĕü-mah)* his last. —*GNB*

> Then Jesus cried out with a loud voice again and died. —*ISV*

The *ISV* translation removes reference to *p-nĕü-mah* and states what happened after Jesus' *last breath.*

Compare the following three translations of the first clause of Luke 8:55, and notice how the *GNB* and *CEV* change "spirit" to "life":

> So her spirit *(p-nĕü-mah)* returned, and she got up at once. —*ISV*

> Her life *(p-nĕü-mah)* returned, and she got up at once. —*GNB*

> She came back to life *(p-nĕü-mah)* and got right up. —*CEV*

Without *p-nĕü-mah* there is no life. Notice a literal, word-for-word translation of the first clause of Luke 8:55:

καὶ [and] ἐπέστρεψεν [returned] τὸ [the] πνεῦμα [breath] αὐτῆς [of her], καὶ [and] ἀνέστη [stand up] παραχρῆμα [immediately].

> *Holmes, Michael W., The Greek New Testament: SBL Edition (Lexham Press; Society of Biblical Literature, 2011–2013), Luke 8:55a.*

Translated in English with proper word order:

> And her breath returned, and she stood up at once.

We must not assume "her spirit," stated in the *ISV* translation of Luke 8:55, is the disembodied ghost of the girl who died that returns to her flesh. *P-nĕü-mah* does not carry with it a specific personality. If it identifies a spirit "being" like an angel, then the context must state that specifically. In this context it is only the force that brings life to the flesh. This must be the only conclusion when we consider the Hebrew understanding of what happens at death, as revealed in Psalm 146:

> Don't put your trust in princes, each a son of man in whom there is no help. His spirit *(roo'-ahkh)* departs, and he returns to the earth. In that very day, his thoughts perish. *—Psalm 146: 3, 4 WEB*

The lack of conscious thought after death is contrary to the idea of a disembodied human existing in the spirit realm, and is why Solomon wrote the following:

> Whoever is joined to all the living has hope. After all, even a live dog is better than a dead lion! For the living know that they will die, but the dead do not know anything. *—Ecclesiastes 9: 4, 5 LEB*

This is in harmony with Yahweh's proclamation to Adam:

> By the sweat of your brow you shall eat bread, until your return to the ground. For from it you were taken; for you are dust, and to dust you shall return. *—Genesis 3:19 LEB*

Because we are all Adam's offspring, we suffer death like he did, and we return to the ground like he did. Before Adam was created, he did not exist (See Understanding Soul). Before we were conceived in the womb, we did not exist. When he died, Adam ceased to exist ("For you are dust, and to dust you shall return.").

When we die, we cease to exist. This truth is why there is need of a resurrection. It is why Jesus needed to be resurrected. The base meaning of resurrection (ἀνάστασις, *ână-stăsis*), is "a standing up again." This is what happened to the girl mentioned in Luke 8:55; she died and was resurrected. Her breath came back and she "stood up," (ἀνέστη, ăn-ĕs-tĕ).

3. Spirit as Words Spoken and Heard

At John 6:63 Jesus says: "The words that I have spoken to you are spirit and are life." *(LEB).* To understand why Jesus made this statement, we will review the highlights of what he said beginning at John 6:47:

> "I most solemnly say to you, whoever believes in me possesses eternal life. I am the bread that gives life. . . . I am this living bread that has come down out of heaven. If anyone eats this bread, he will live forever, and the bread that I will give for the life of the world is my own flesh."
> But the Jews kept on wrangling with one another and saying, "How can He give us His flesh to eat?" Then Jesus said to them, "I most solemnly say to you, unless you eat the flesh of the Son of Man and drink His blood, you do not have life in you."
> . . . So many of His disciples, when they heard it, said, "This teaching is hard to take in. Who can listen to it?" But as Jesus naturally knew that His disciples were grumbling about this, He said to them, "Is this shocking to you? . . . The Spirit is what gives life; the flesh does not help at all. *The truths that I have told you are spirit and life." —John 6:47,48,51-53, 59-61, 63 WNT (emphasis mine)*

Jesus used the "bread that has come down out of heaven" as a metaphor for his future sacrifice. He was not being literal. This is similar to the statement, "Man will not live on bread alone, but on every word that comes out of the mouth of God." (Matthew 4:4 LEB, Compare Deuteronomy 8:3).

Spirit inspired utterance will not sustain our flesh, but can lead people to salvation. If they symbolically *eat* the spiritual food (take into their hearts and minds spiritual instruction), they will gain everlasting life.

In this way, *spirit* (the words spoken by Jesus) gives life, and is more important than fleshly nourishment. Jesus' words are an invisible force (a spiritual wind) that motivates, guides, and corrects us, nudging us onto the path that will lead to our salvation.

> The word "Spirit," here, evidently does not refer to the Holy Spirit, for he adds, "The words that I speak unto you, they are spirit." He refers here, probably, to the doctrine which he had been teaching in opposition to their notions and desires. "My doctrine is spiritual; it is fitted to quicken and nourish the soul [the spiritual life]. It is from heaven. Your doctrine or your views are earthly, and may be called flesh, or fleshly, as pertaining only to the support of the body. You place a great value on the doctrine that Moses fed the body; yet that did not permanently profit, for your fathers are dead. You seek also food from me, but your views and desires are gross and earthly.". . . By this Jesus shows them that he did not intend that his words should be taken literally. . . They are spiritual. They are not to be understood literally. *Barnes, Albert, Notes on the Bible, 1847-1885, John 6:63.*

4. God as Spirit

> God is spirit (*p-nĕü-mah*), and the ones who worship him must worship in spirit (*p-nĕü-mah*) and truth. *—John 16:28 LEB*

Yahweh is spirit, which means he is invisible to humans because he resides in the unseen spiritual realm.

> But he [Yahweh] said, "You are not able to see my face, because a human will not see me and live." —*Exodus 33:20 LEB*

Paul says Jesus is the "image of the invisible God." (Colossians 1:15 LEB). Paul praises Yahweh, saying, "To the King of the ages, immortal, invisible, the only God, be honor and glory forever and ever." (1 Timothy 1:17 ESV).

Whatever form Yahweh has, human flesh cannot exist in his presence. This is supported by the following statements:

> For indeed our God is a consuming fire. *—Hebrews 12:29 LEB*

> But I say this, brothers, that flesh and blood is not able to inherit the kingdom of God, nor can corruption inherit incorruptibility. *—1 Corinthians 15:50 LEB*

> To whom can the holy God be compared? Is there anyone else like him? Look up at the sky! Who created the stars you see? The one who leads them out like an army, he knows how many there are and calls each one by name! His power is so great—not one of them is ever missing! *—Isaiah 40:25,26 GNB*

To worship "in spirit" means we must worship accurately (in harmony with God's will), with our heart; with a dominating mental attitude, as opposed to relying on traditions, rituals, and physical locations. We can connect to God from anywhere, although He resides in a specific place in heaven.

> For Christ did not enter into a sanctuary made by hands, a mere copy of the true one, but into heaven itself, now to appear in the presence of God on our behalf. —*Hebrews 9:24 LEB*

5. Heavenly Beings as Spirit

> And concerning the angels he says, "The one who makes his angels winds *(p-nĕü-mah)*, and his servants a flame of fire." —*Hebrews 1:7 LEB*

Angels can materialize in human form and be seen by humans, but are not by nature material or fleshly. Their normal state of existence is invisible to humans; they are spirit beings. They are actively alive and can exert great power, so the terms *roo'-ahkh* and *p-nĕü-mah* are appropriate descriptions for them.

> . . . the angels are the "attendant servants" of God . . . "Flame of fire." This probably refers to lightning —which is often the meaning of the phrase. The word "ministers" [servants] here, means the same as angels, and the sense of the whole is, that the attending retinue of God, when he manifests himself with great power and glory, is like the winds and the lightning. His angels are like them. They are prompt to do his will - rapid, quick, obedient in his service. *Barnes, Albert, Notes on the Bible, 1847-1885, Hebrews 1:7.*

6. Spirit as Satan and Fallen Angels

At Ephesians 6:11,12 Paul says: "Put on the full armor of God, so that you may be able to stand against the stratagems of the devil, because our struggle is not against blood and flesh, but against the rulers, against the authorities, against the world rulers of this darkness, against the spiritual forces of wickedness in the heavenly places." (LEB)

This does not imply an abstract *spiritual wickedness.* Based on context it refers to a wickedness caused by *spirit beings,* as noted in the following five translations of this verse:

> Array yourselves in the full armour of God, so that you may stand up to the artfulness of the Adversary. For we are not contending with mortals but with angelic Rulers and Authorities, with the Overlords of the Dark State, the spirit forces of evil in the heavenly spheres. —*ONT*

> Put on all the armour which God provides, so that you may be able to stand firm against the devices of the devil. For our fight is not against human foes, but against cosmic powers, against the authorities and potentates of this dark world, against the superhuman forces of evil in the heavens. —*NEB*

> Array yourselves in the armour-panoply that God supplies, that you may be able to hold your post unflinchingly against the Devil's stratagems. For we have to close in grapple not with human flesh and blood alone, but with the Principalities, with Powers, with the Lords of Darkness whose present sway is world-wide, with the spirit-host of Wicked Beings that haunt the upper air. —*WAY*

> Put on God's armour, in order that you may be able to make a stand against the devil's stratagems. We are not fighting against human enemies, but against the rulers and the authorities, against the world-rulers of this dark age, against the spirit-forces of evil in the supernatural world. —*TTNT*

> Put on the complete armour of God, so as to be able to stand firm against all the stratagems of the devil. For ours is not a conflict with mere flesh and blood, but with the despotisms, the empires, the forces that control and govern this dark world—the spiritual hosts of evil arrayed against us in the heavenly warfare. —*NTMS*

While the words in the above translations vary, the meaning is consistent; the world of humankind is ruled by wicked spirit beings. This is in harmony with the OT view of how the gentile nations were created. Deuteronomy 32 explains how Yahweh transferred his oversight of humankind to the Sons of God, after scattering the people by confusing their language (See Genesis 11:5-9).

Note the following five translations of Deuteronomy 32:8,9:

> When the Most High was apportioning nations, as he scattered Adam's sons, he fixed boundaries of nations according to the number of divine sons, and his people Iakob became the Lord's portion, Israel a measured part of his inheritance. —*NETS*

> When the Most High gave the nations their inheritance, when he divided up humankind, he set the boundaries of the peoples, according to the number of the heavenly assembly. For the LORD's

> allotment is his people, Jacob is his special possession. —*NET*

> When the Most High divided the nations, when he separated the sons of Adam, he set the bounds of the nations according to the number of the angels of God. And his people Jacob became the portion of the Lord, Israel was the line of his inheritance. —*BES*

> When the Most High gave to the nations their inheritance, when he divided mankind, he fixed the borders of the peoples according to the number of the sons of God. But the LORD's portion is his people, Jacob his allotted heritage. —*ESV*

> The Most High assigned nations their lands; he determined where peoples should live. He assigned to each nation a heavenly being, but Jacob's descendants he chose for himself. —*GNB*

Many OT translations have "sons (children) of Israel," instead of "sons of God" for the apportioning of boundaries for the nations. Yet this could not have been an option at the time of the scattering, because Israel did not exist at that time. Abram had just been selected by Yahweh to be the father of his favored nation, so the "sons (children) of Israel" version is a later corruption to the Hebrew text of Deuteronomy. The translations based on the Greek Septuagint, *NETS* and *BES*, preserve the original wording, which a few Hebrew-based translations also adopt based on context and logic.

This apportioning of nations to the Sons of God is the reason for Yahweh's anger in Psalm 82:

> God presides in the heavenly council; in the assembly of the gods he gives his decision: "You must stop judging unjustly; you must no longer be partial to the wicked!
> . . . How ignorant you are! How stupid! You are completely corrupt, and justice has disappeared from the world. 'You are gods,' I said; 'all of you are children of the Most High.' But you will die like mortals; your life will end like that of any prince."
> —*Psalm 82: 1,2,5-7 GNB*

The proclamation "you will die like mortals" or "You will die like men," (LEB), or "Like the earth-born, ye shall die" (TEB), is significant because no heavenly beings *(elohim)* had died up to that point. Death is the punishment for all disobedient, whether human or *elohim*. (See The Justice of God.)

As Paul said in his letter to the Ephesians, Christians must resist the wicked spiritual oversight that has corrupted the world. They can do this by drawing close to God and focusing on his spiritual influence. (Compare Ephesians 2:2; John 12:31; Ephesians 4:30; 6:11; Acts 26:18; 2 Corinthians 4:4; Colossians 1:13).

The Holy Ghost

The occurrences of both רוּחַ (roo'-ahkh) and πνεῦμα (*p-nĕü-mah*) to describe God's spirit (his holy spirit) outnumber every other use of the terms.

Not until the 4th-century C.E. was the term "Holy Ghost" identified as part of the "Godhead" that became the official Christian doctrine of the Trinity within the Roman Empire.

> The trinity of God is defined by the Church as the belief that in God are three persons who subsist in one nature. The belief as so defined was reached

> only in the 4th and 5th centuries AD and hence is not explicitly and formally a biblical belief. The trinity of persons within the unity of nature is defined in terms of "person" and "nature" which are GK philosophical terms; actually, the terms do not appear in the Bible. The trinitarian definitions arose as a result of long controversies in which these terms and others such as "essence" and "substance" were erroneously applied to God by some theologians. *McKenzie, S.J., John L., 1965, Dictionary of the Bible, page 899, paragraph 2.*

Contrary to the trinitarian belief, the scriptures communicate the consistent understanding that *holy spirit* is the means by which Yahweh accomplishes his purpose and executes his will, either by his direct intervention, or by spirit beings sent by Yahweh to accomplish specific tasks. (See 1 Kings 22:21,22; Numbers 11:25; Isaiah 11:2; 42:5.)

Yahweh is spirit (invisible) and holy. All faithful heavenly beings (Sons of God), are spirit and holy. If the "Holy Ghost" is a heavenly being of status equal to Yahweh, there should be in scripture a proper name to distinguish such a spirit being from all other spirit beings; Holy Ghost (or Holy Spirit) is a title, not a proper name. We are told the names of prominent spirit beings in scripture: Yahweh, Michael, Gabriel, (and Raphael in the apocryphal *Book of Tobit*, which is included in some translations).[4] The "Holy Ghost" who is considered a person equal to Yahweh, a member of the trinitarian Godhead, is nameless.

Knowing the importance Yahweh places on proper names (see Clarifying the Name of God), the lack of a proper name for the "Holy

---

4. Satan (from the Hebrew שָׂטָן, *sấṭấn*, meaning "accuser" or "adversary", is derived from a verb meaning primarily "to obstruct, oppose"), and Devil, the English word for the Greek, διάβολος, diabŏlŏs, (a slanderer), are titles and not proper names. In Job and Zechariah the term "Satan" is preceded by the definite article ה, *ha* (the), and is properly rendered, "the Satan."

Ghost" is not in harmony with scripture, and therefore is evidence of a non-biblical source for the doctrine. Please note: Proverbs 30:4 only asks about two proper names, not three.

Spirit Personified

Many Christians view the personified spirit in John 14:16 as a reference to the Holy Ghost, the third member of the Trinity.

The personification of inanimate things is not an unusual literary convention. Paul personified *sin*, *death*, and God's *mercy* as "reigning" like kings over humankind, yet these three things are not actual persons. (See Romans 5:14,17, 21; 6:12.)

Jesus is quoted personifying spirit as a παράκλητος, *paráklĕtos* (a helper, advocate, comforter) at John 14:16. No proper name for the "Spirit of Truth" is revealed by Jesus, which may indicate it is either referring only to spiritual (invisible) *influence* over the faithful (an *internal attitude* cultivated in each Christian), or the assignment given to an unnamed angel sent to help the faithful understand God's will.

Spirit - What Gender Do We Call It?

Like other Indo-European languages, Greek has three genders of nouns: Masculine, Feminine, and Neuter. There is little logic behind the genders assigned to nouns, which is true in many Indo-European languages.

German	English	Greek
Die Tür (Feminine)	The Door	ἡ πόρτα (Feminine)
Das Fenster (Neuter)	The Window	τό παράθυρο (Neuter)
Der Tisch (Masculine)	The Table	ή τράπεζα (Feminine)
Der Geist (Masculine)	The Spirit	τό πνεύμα (Neuter)

Grammatical rules insist pronouns conform to the gender of the noun to which they refer. This is the case in John 14:16 where Jesus calls the spirit *pará-klētos.* The noun is masculine, so the pronouns are *he/him.* Spirit, as shown above, is neuter in Greek, so the proper pronouns are *it/its.* Most translations ignore the standard grammatical rules and instead continue using masculine pronouns in Verse 17.

> 16 And I will ask the Father, and *he*[1] will give you another Advocate *(pará-klētos)*, in order that *he*[2] may be with you forever—
> 17 the Spirit of truth, whom the world is not able to receive, because it does not see *him*[3] or know *him*[4]. You know *him*[5], because *he*[6] resides with you and will be in you. —*John 14:16, 17 LEB*

The Pronouns:

#1 in verse 16 refers to "the Father."

#2 in verse 16 is understood by many to refer to "the Advocate" (it can also refer to "the Father").

Both #1 and #2 pronouns are not in the Greek text, they are implied as part of the verbs used, which are both third person singular verbs. The pronouns are written in the masculine gender in English because the nouns are masculine.

#3 in verse 17, αὐτὸ, (it) third person, accusative, singular, neuter.

#4 is not in the Greek text and is supplied from context in the English translation.

#5 αὐτὸ, (it) third person, accusative, singular, neuter.

#6 is not in the Greek text and is implied as part of

> the verb used, which is active, indicative, third person singular.

The *LEB* translation is like other translations that use masculine pronouns in verse 17. The word *pará-klĕtos* is masculine, so any direct reference is also masculine, but gender is not inherited from noun to noun. A neuter noun is always neuter and so are its associated pronouns.

To avoid the pronoun issues, the *Literal Standard Version* took a paraphrased path in English that still follows the Greek, but without the masculine pronouns in verse 17.

> 17 the Spirit of truth, whom the world is not able to receive, because it does not see nor know this One, and you know this One, because this One remains with you, and will be in you. —*John 14:17 LSV*

The LSV version is an example of when dogma triumphs over the truth—the Scriptures are translated to fit orthodox belief. By saying "you know this One," (and capitalizing the word, One), the *LSV* implies the spirit of truth is the Holy Ghost; God's titles are capitalized, so by capitalizing "One" the *LSV* implies Godhead identity. Reading verses 16 and 17 in Greek does not assign Godhead identity to the spirit of truth.

Rotherham's *The Emphasized Bible,* while using archaic English verbs, has a more accurate translation of the original Greek (I have removed the pronunciation marks that intersect the original printing):

> 16 And I will request the Father, and another Advocate will he give unto you, That he may be with you age-abidingly, —
> 17 The Spirit of truth, — Which the world cannot receive, Because it beholdeth it not, nor getteth to know it. But ye are getting to know it; Because with

> you it abideth, And in you it is. *Joseph Bryant Rotherham, 1897, The Emphasized Bible: A Translation Designed to Set Forth the Exact Meaning, the Proper Terminology, and the Graphic Style of the Sacred Original (Bellingham, WA: Logos Research Systems, Inc., 2010), John 14:16–17.*

So we are left with these possibilities:

1. The spirit of truth is an invisible spirit being who is sent to support Christians in a similar way an invisible spirit being was sent by Yahweh to influence King Ahab.
2. The spirit of truth is not a spirit being, but a supernatural expression used to influence our minds and direct us through the muck of worldly concepts toward the truth revealed in God's word.

Both possibilities are acceptable, independently or combined, while neither support the belief that the spirit of truth is the third person of the Trinity, the Holy Ghost equal to Yahweh.

Spirit is "In" Someone

> So then, see that Yahweh has placed a false spirit in the mouth of all of these your prophets, and Yahweh has spoken disaster concerning you. —*1 Kings 22:23* LEB

> Create a clean heart for me, O God, and renew a steadfast spirit within me. —*Psalm 51:10 LEB*

> And I will give to them one heart, and a new spirit I will give in their inner parts. —*Ezekiel 11:19 LEB*

> Be renewed in the spirit of your mind. —*Ephesians 4:23 LEB*

> And I have heard that a spirit of the gods is in you and enlightenment and insight and excellent wisdom was found in you. —*Daniel 5:14 LEB*

The spirit that is "in" someone is a mental disposition, whether encouraged by external influence, or born from our own thoughts.

Spirit is "On" Someone

> Then the Spirit of Yahweh came upon Jahaziel, the son of Zechariah, the son of Benaiah, the son of Jeiel, the son of Mattaniah, the Levite from the descendants of Asaph, in the midst of the assembly. *2 Chronicles 20:14 LEB*

> Look! here is my servant; I hold him, my chosen one, in whom my soul delights. I have put my spirit on him; he will bring justice forth to the nations. —*Isaiah 42:1 LEB (compare Matthew 12:18)*

> And the Holy Spirit[5] came down upon him in the form of a dove. A voice from heaven said, "You are my own dear Son, and I am pleased with you." —*Luke 3:22 LEB*

The spirit "came upon Jahaziel," which means he was overshadowed by Yahweh's influence. The same is true in Isaiah 42 where Yahweh says, "I have put my spirit on him," which

---

5. The words *spirit* and *holy spirit* are often capitalized in English translations due to the dogma of the Trinity. The words are not capitalized in the original Greek text (see any Greek text).

indicates Yahweh's favor, and unity with regard to his purpose; "he will bring justice forth to the nations."

In Luke the holy spirit is the means by which Yahweh spoke to his son; "my own dear Son, and I am pleased with you."

Since no man can see God and live (compare Exodus 33:20), the only way Yahweh can communicate with humans is via spirit.

Spirit is "Given"

> When the last days come, I will give my Spirit to everyone. Your sons and daughters will prophesy. Your young men will see visions, and your old men will have dreams. —*Acts 2:17 LEB*

> But Christ lives in you. So you are alive because God has accepted you, even though your bodies must die because of your sins. Yet God raised Jesus to life! God's Spirit now lives in you, and he will raise you to life by his Spirit. —*Romans 8:10,11 LEB*

When given God's spirit, when it is "in" us, or "on" us, humans are not possessed by another individual. Spirit (the tool Yahweh uses to accomplish his purpose), imparts to the faithful various gifts from Yahweh and eventually everlasting life.

When Christ lives "in" us, he is in our hearts and minds as we strive to reflect his faith. This unity of purpose draws us closer to Yahweh and we benefit from his mercy because of the ransom of his son.

Underlying each use of *spirit* (in Hebrew and Greek) is the root understanding of an invisible force (like wind or breath) that can be witnessed and felt, whether an internal (mental) disposition; the force that activates life through breathing; or an external manifestation of power that creates change—either through humans, heavenly beings (both good and bad), or through direct intervention by Yahweh.

Chapter 10

Understanding Soul

The word *soul* in Modern English has many meanings:

1. Nonphysical aspect of person: regarded as distinct from the physical body.
2. Feelings: a person's emotional and moral nature.
3. Spirit surviving death: in some systems of religious belief, the spiritual part of a human being that is believed to continue to exist after the body dies.
4. Spiritual depth: either in a person or in something created by a person, e.g. Though technically perfect, the drawing lacked soul.
5. Essence: what gives somebody or something a distinctive character, e.g. In my travels I hoped to discover the soul of the Lakota people.
6. Type of person: especially one regarded sympathetically or with familiarity, e.g. Poor soul!
7. Anyone: anyone at all, e.g. You have to promise not to tell a soul.
8. An individual person, e.g. A country of 10 million souls.

9. Perfect example of a positive quality, i.e. The hotel manager was the soul of discretion.

Hebrew Soul

Hebrew uses נפש, *nephesh* (singular), נפשתי, *naphshote* (plural), to indicate the personal soul, or personal life that the soul experiences. *Nephesh*, originally *breath*, indicates:

1. The emotional life.
2. Is used as a strong personal or reflexive pronoun, i.e. "myself."
3. Is equivalent to the terms *person, creature, animal, beast.*

Underlying each application of the word *nephesh* is the reference to the individual being, or each member of a specific class of being.

> So God created the great sea creatures and every living *creature (nephesh)* that moves, with which the waters swarm, according to their kinds, and every winged bird according to its kind . . . And God said, "Let the earth bring forth living *creatures (nephesh)* according to their kinds—livestock and creeping things and beasts of the earth according to their kinds." And it was so. —*Genesis 1:21,24 ESV (emphasis mine)*

> So then Yahweh God formed man [of the] dust of the ground, and breathed in his nostrils the breath of life—and man became a *living soul (nephesh)*. —*Genesis 2:7 TEB (emphasis mine)*

Adam became a *living soul*, so the opposite must also be possible, a *nonliving or dead soul.* This eventually happened when Adam's potential for everlasting life was removed by Yahweh, and Adam died.

> But from the tree of the knowledge of good and evil you shall not eat, for in the day that you eat from it you shall surely die. —*Genesis 2:17 LEB*

To fully appreciate the intent behind the term נפש *(nephesh)*, replace any English words used in translations for *nephesh* with the English word *soul.*

1. Souls Die

> Behold, all *souls (naphshote)* are mine; the *soul (nephesh)* of the father as well as the *soul (nephesh)* of the son is mine: the *soul (nephesh)* who sins shall die. —*Ezekiel 18:4 ESV*

> When a man is found stealing any *person (nephesh)* from among his brethren of the sons of Israel, and making merchandise of him or selling him, then shall that thief die. —*Deuteronomy 24:7 TEB (emphasis mine)*

The "thief" mentioned in Deuteronomy 24:7 is a person—a *nephesh*—a soul who shall die.

> Let my life *(nephesh)* die the death of an upright person. —*Numbers 23:10b LEB*

2. Soul not the Same as Spirit

Who doesn't know that in all these, Yahweh's hand has done this, in whose hand is the *life (nephesh)* of every living thing, and the *breath (roo'ahkh)* of all mankind? *—Job 12:9,10 JPS*

3. Soul Needs Breath to be Alive

So that my *soul (nephesh)* chooses strangling, death rather than my bones. *—Job 7:15 WEB*

They struck all the *souls (naphshote)* who were in it with the edge of the sword, utterly destroying them. There was no one left who breathed. He burned Hazor with fire. *—Joshua 11:11 WEB*

4. Soul has Blood

And surely your blood of your *lives (naphshote)* will I require; at the hand of every beast will I require it; and at the hand of man, even at the hand of every man's brother, will I require the *life (nephesh)* of man. *—Genesis 9:5 JPS*

Also in thy skirts is found the blood of the *souls (naphshote)* of the innocent poor. *—Jeremiah 2:34 JPS*

Her princes in the midst thereof are like wolves ravening the prey: to shed blood, and to destroy *souls (naphshote)*, so as to get dishonest gain. *—Ezekiel 22: 27 JPS*

5. Soul as Reflexive Pronoun

My *soul (nephesh)* weeps because of grief; strengthen me according to your word. *—Psalm 119:28 LEB*

I will greatly rejoice in Yahweh! My *soul (nephesh)* will be joyful in my God; for he has clothed me with the garments of salvation. *—Isaiah 61:10 WEB*

6. Soul as Life

And it came to pass, when they had brought them forth abroad, that he said: "Escape for thy *life (nephesh)*; look not behind thee, neither stay thou in all the Plain; escape to the mountain, lest thou be swept away." *—Genesis 19:17 JPS*

But whoever beats an animal to death is to replace it, *life (nephesh)* for *life (nephesh)*. *—Leviticus 24:18 ISV*

For my father fought for you and risked his *life (nephesh),* and delivered you from the hand of Midian. *—Judges 9:17 ESV*

Greek Soul

Like the Hebrew word נפשׁ *(nephesh),* the Greek ψυχή, *p-soo-khay* (singular), ψυχαί, *p-soo-khai* (plural), refers to the individual being, or each member of a specific class of being, and the life they experience.

1. Humans are Souls

Thus also it is written, "The first man, Adam, became a living *soul,"* *(p-soo-khay). —1 Corinthians 15:45 LEB*

God waited in the days of Noah, while an ark was being constructed, in which a few—that is, eight *souls (p-soo-khai)*—were rescued through water. *—1 Peter 3:20 LEB*

2. Souls Die

And he said to them, "My *soul (p-soo-khay)* is deeply grieved, to the point of death. Remain here and stay awake." *—Mark 14:34 LEB*

And it will be that every *soul (p-soo-khay)* who does not listen to that prophet will be destroyed utterly from the people. *—Acts 3:23 LEB*

Then Jesus said to them,"I ask you, is it lawful to do good on the Sabbath or to do evil, to save a life *(p-soo-khay)* or to destroy it?" *—Luke 6:9 NET*

3. Animals are Souls Who Die

And the second poured out his bowl into the sea; and it became blood as of a dead man; and every living *soul (p-soo-khay)* died, even the things that were in the sea. *—Revelation 16:3 ASV*

4. Soul not the Same as Spirit

For the word of God is living and active and sharper than any double-edged sword, and piercing as far as the division of *soul (p-soo-khay)* and *spirit (p-nĕü-mah)*, both joints and marrow, and able to judge the reflections and thoughts of the heart. *—Hebrews 4:12 LEB*

Now may the God of peace himself sanctify you completely, and may your *spirit (p-nĕü-mah)* and *soul (p-soo-khay)* and body be kept complete, blameless at the coming of our Lord Jesus Christ. *—1 Thessalonians 5:23 LEB*

5. Soul Sometimes Refers to Life

For whoever wants to save his *life (p-soo-khay)* will lose it, but whoever loses his life *(p-soo-khay)* on account of me will find it. —Matthew 16:25 LEB (compare Luke 9:24)

6. Soul May Refer to Future Life

Don't be afraid of those who kill the body, but are not able to kill the soul *(p-soo-khay).* Rather, fear him who is able to destroy both soul *(p-soo-khay)* and body in Gehenna. —Matthew 10:28 WEB

By your patient endurance you will gain your lives *(p-soo-khai).* —Luke 21:19 LEB

7. Deliverance of Dead Souls from The Grave

For thou wilt not abandon my soul *(p-soo-khay)* to the Place of Death, nor surrender me, your holy one, to undergo corruption—Acts 2:27 20CNT

Because you will not abandon me (*p-soo-khay)* in the world of the dead; you will not allow your faithful servant to rot in the grave. —Acts 2:27 GNB

For you will not forsake my soul *(p-soo-khay)* to Hades, Nor will you let your Holy One experience decay. —Acts 2:27 WNT

Part Two

Who is Jesus?

The following chapters contain statements that reveal how the first-century authors viewed Jesus. Keep in mind, all these writings were completed after Jesus died, by men who knew Jesus (Matthew, John, Peter, James, and Jude), and men who faithfully proclaimed the Good News (Paul, Mark, and Luke).

For God so loved the world, that he gave his one and only Son, that whoever believes in him should not perish, but have eternal life.

—John 3:16 LEB

Chapter 11

Jesus in the Gospels

> **Matthew 3:17:** And behold, there was a voice from heaven saying, "This is my beloved Son, with whom I am well pleased." —*LEB* (See also Mark 1:11, Luke 3:22.)

The voice from Heaven declares Jesus is the Son of God, with whom God is pleased. No mention is made of Jesus being God in any form.

> **Matthew 4:1-10:** Then Jesus was led up into the wilderness by the Spirit to be tempted by the devil, and after he had fasted forty days and forty nights, then he was hungry. And the tempter approached and said to him, "If you are the Son of God, order that these stones become bread." But he answered and said, "It is written, 'Man will not live on bread alone, but on every word that comes out of the mouth of God.'" Then the devil took him to the holy city and placed him on the highest point of the temple and said to him, "If you are the Son of God, throw yourself down! For it is written, 'He will command his angels concerning you,' and 'On their

> hands they will lift you up, lest you strike your foot against a stone.'" Jesus said to him, "On the other hand it is written, 'You are not to put the Lord your God to the test.'" Again, the devil took him to a very high mountain and showed him all the kingdoms of the world and their glory, and he said to him, "I will give to you all these things, if you will fall down and worship me." Then Jesus said to him, "Go away, Satan, for it is written, 'You shall worship the Lord your God and serve only him.'" *—LEB* (See also Mark 1:12,13, Luke 4:1-13.)

After this the devil leaves, but only until another opportune time to test Jesus, as recorded by Luke:

> And when the devil had completed every temptation, he departed from him until a favorable time. *—Luke 4: 13 LEB.*

Can the devil tempt God? Can God do evil things? James says, "No one who is being tempted should say, 'I am being tempted by God,' for God cannot be tempted by evil, and he himself tempts no one." (See James 1:13 LEB.)

Jesus kept his integrity to God and did not fall to the Devil's temptations. If Jesus was God, Satan would not have considered trying to tempt him because "God cannot be tempted by evil."

The devil says to Jesus, "If you are the Son of God," (Matthew 4:3 LEB), identifying Jesus as a person who is a creation of God, not God himself.

The devil quotes Psalm 91:11, 12, "He (Yahweh) will command his angels concerning you," and "On their hands they will lift you up, lest you strike your foot against a stone." (ESV) So Satan implies that God (Yahweh) would have his angels save Jesus. If Jesus was God, could he not save himself?

The devil offers Jesus a Kingdom for an act of worship (Matthew 4:9). The Almighty God has authority over everything, so He could not be tempted to worship someone to acquire authority. Jesus, a son of God, could be tempted, just as Adam (who was also a son of God) was tempted. (Compare Luke 3:38).

> **Matthew 6:8,9:** Don't be like them. Your Father knows what you need before you ask. You should pray like this: "Our Father in heaven, help us to honor your name." —*CEV*

Jesus identifies the Father as the one who hears our prayers. By doing this he emphasized the Father above himself. We are to pray to God ("Our Father"), not to Jesus. Jesus is the mediator between God and men (1 Timothy 2:5). We are to pray through Jesus to God.

> **Mark 10:18:** So Jesus said to him, "Why do you call me good? No one is good except God alone." —*LEB*

The most important phrase in this verse is, "No one is good," because Jesus included himself in that group by asking, "Why do you call me good?" It is obvious from the various accounts of Christians being called "good" that Jesus was not saying only God can be called "good." Jesus said he was the Good Shepard, and he called other people good (Matthew 5:45; 12:35; John 10:11). In this verse, Jesus stated he was not God by his remark that only God is good; good in the purest sense. Jesus, and all humans, can only be a reflection (an image) of God's goodness and therefore will never exemplify goodness to the same level as Yahweh.

> **Mark 10:40:** ". . .but to sit at my right hand or at my left is not mine to grant, but is for those for whom it has been prepared." —*LEB*

Mark quotes Jesus, who admits his authority is limited. Only the Father has authority to grant positions in his Kingdom.

> **Mark 13:32,33:** No one knows the day or the time. The angels in heaven don't know, and the Son himself doesn't know. Only the Father knows. So watch out and be ready! You don't know when the time will come. —*CEV* (Compare Matthew 24:36)

Jesus admits his authority is limited. Only the Father knows. This is not because of Jesus being restricted to the Earth during this time period. Only the Father is in control of times and seasons. (Compare Psalm 110:1; Daniel 2:21).

> **Luke 9:20:** And he (Jesus) said to them, "But who do you say that I am?" And Peter answered and said, "The Christ of God." —*LEB*

The word Christ is from the Greek, χριστός (chris-tos) which is the Greek translation of the Hebrew word for Messiah, and means "anointed one." So by saying, "The Christ of God," Peter was proclaiming Jesus to be "the anointed."

> **Luke 10:22:** "All things have been handed over to me by my Father." —*LEB*

In this verse, Luke quotes Jesus, and Jesus says his Father gave him "all things." This one statement alone indicates Jesus is not Almighty God, because Yahweh cannot be given what he already has, but he can delegate authority to someone who does not already have it.

> **John 1:1:** In the beginning was the Word, and the Word was with God, and the Word was God. —*LEB*

This is one of the most misinterpreted verses in the Bible. John was schooled in Hebrew theology. He knew that Yahweh was not part of a pagan trinity of gods, as were many of the gods of the gentile nations surrounding Israel. (See End Note #1)

He also knew the Hebrew words for "god" identified different inhabitants of the spirit realm: members of the Heavenly Council; angels and demons; and Yahweh himself. He knew Jesus had existed in the heavens before Mary gave birth to him. He knew Jesus had been sent by Yahweh to be the Messiah, the Son of Man, who would be the Savior of Adam's offspring through his death and resurrection. John also knew that Jesus, in his pre-human existence, had been alongside Yahweh before the creation of Adam. Everything Yahweh made was made through his son, the Word of God, who is revealed in Proverbs 8 as the personified Wisdom of God.

> "I, wisdom, live with prudence, and I find knowledge and discretion. . . Yahweh possessed me, the first of his ways, before his acts of old. From eternity, I was set up from the first, from the beginning of the earth. When there were no depths, I was brought forth, when there were no springs of abounding water. Before mountains had been shaped, before hills, I was brought forth. When he had not yet made earth and fields, or the first dust of the world, when he established the heavens, there I was, when he drew a circle upon the face of the deep, when he made skies from above, when he founded fountains of the deep, when he assigned his limits to the sea, that waters shall not transgress his command, when he marked the foundations of the earth, I was beside him, a master workman, and I was delighting day by day, rejoicing before him always, rejoicing in the world of his earth, and my delight was with the

> children of humankind." —*Proverbs 8:12,22-31 LEB* (Compare 1 Corinthians 8:6).

Note that the personified *Wisdom* was "brought forth." (8:24) The WEB, NET and BBE say, "I was born." This *Wisdom* calls himself a "master workman." (8:30) ISV, NET, WEB say "master craftsman."

John, because he understood all the background theology regarding the Messiah, the one sent by Yahweh, he wrote, "and god (thĕ-ŏs) was the word." He did this because in his Hebrew mind all inhabitants of the spirit realm are *elohim*. The construction of the entire verse bares witness to John's usage of the term.

A word for word Greek to English translation of John 1:1:

Ἐν [In] ἀρχῇ [beginning] ἦν [was] ὁ [the] λόγος [word], καὶ [and] ὁ [the] λόγος [word] ἦν [was] πρὸς [with] τὸν [the] θεόν [god], καὶ [and] θεὸς [god] ἦν [was] ὁ [the] λόγος [word].

Holmes, Michael W., The Greek New Testament: SBL Edition (Lexham Press; Society of Biblical Literature, 2011–2013), John 1:1

Notice the lack of the definite article (the) before the last "god." This makes the phrase "and god" a predicate phrase, which describes an attribute of the following noun, "the word."

> We reach a more difficult issue in the Gospel of John. Here, in the prologue, the Word is said to be God, but, as often observed, in contrast with the clause, "the Word was with God," the definite article is not used (in the final clause). For this reason, it is generally translated "and the Word was divine" or is not regarded as God in the absolute sense of the

name. *The New English Bible* neatly paraphrases the phrase in the words, "and what God was, the Word was." In a second passage in the prologue (1:18) the textual evidence attests "only-begotten God" more strongly than "only-begotten Son", but the latter is preferred by many commentators as being more in harmony with Johannine usage and with the succeeding clause, "who is in the bosom of the Father." In neither passage is Jesus unequivocally called God, while again and again in the Gospel he is named "the Son" or "the Son of God". *Taylor, Vincent, The Expository Times, January 1962, page 117.*

In the words of Jesus and in much of the rest of the NT the God of Israel (GK ho theos) is the Father of Jesus Christ. It is for this reason that the title "ho theos," which now designates the Father as the personal reality, is not applied in the NT to Jesus himself. Jesus is the Son of God (of ho theos) . . . John 1:1 should rigorously be translated "the word was with the God [the Father], and the word was a divine being. *McKenzie, S.J., John L., 1965, Dictionary of the Bible, page 317, paragraph 5.*

AND THE WORD WAS GOD, more lit. "And a God (i.e. a Divine Being) was the Word." *Young, Robert, Concise Commentary on the Holy Bible, 1865, page 54.*

Here "God" is used predicatively, without the article. The Word, whom he has just distinguished from thc Person of God, is nevertheless a divine person in his own right. *Vawter, Bruce, The Four Gospels: An Introduction, 1967, page 38.*

> Jn 1:1 The Word was with God and shared his nature. Literally the Greek may be translated, "The Word was with the God and God was the word." There is a distinction in the Greek here between "the God" and "God." In the first instance the article is used and this makes the reference specific. In the second instance there is no article and it is difficult to believe that the omission is not significant. In effect it gives an adjectival quality to the second use of theos (god) so that the phrase means "The Word was divine." *The Translators New Testament, British and Foreign Bible Society, 1973, page 451.*

Romans 9:5 has a phrase similar to John 1:1:

> Christ would not be equated absolutely with God, but only described as a being of divine nature, for the word "theos" has no article. *Brown, Colin, New International Dictionary of New Testament Theology, 1975, Vol 2, pg. 80.*

Acts 28:6 also parallels John 1:1, with exactly the same predicate construction. But the majority of English versions translate it not, "He was God", but, "he was a god." (See AMP, ASV, BBE, CEV, ESV, GNB, ISV, KJV, LEB, LSV, NET, TTNT, WEB, WNT, and YLT. The ECT says "an elohim.") With equal justification from the Greek text, John 1:1 should be rendered: "And the word was a god," or "the word was divine."

> **John 1:14:** The Word became a human being and, full of grace and truth, lived among us. We saw his glory, the glory which he received as the Father's only Son. —*GNB*

In what sense was Jesus the Father's only son? Or as in other translations, the only-begotten Son?

The word *only* is an adverb used to indicate the one thing or person that solely or exclusively is involved in a situation. *Begotten* is the past participle of the verb *beget*, which means to bring about, create, produce with reference to a father of a child. So an only-begotten son would be a person solely or exclusively produced by their father, an only child.

The Greek terms have the same meaning. The term used in the verse is μονογενοῦς (mŏnŏgĕnous), the genitive, singular, masculine form of μονογενής (mŏnŏgĕnās), which is a combination of the roots μόνος (mŏnŏs), one, only, first, and γίνομαι (gĭnŏmai), be, become, born. So a literal *only-born,* or *first-born.*

Since the above meanings are obvious when used regarding people, why should we understand something different when referring to Jesus?

God is the source of creation: "one God, the Father, *of whom* (ἐξ οὗ, *ĕx hou*: out of whom) are all things." Jesus is the Agent or Instrument through whom God created: "and there is one Lord, Jesus Christ, *through whom* (δί οὗ, *dĭ hou*: by the instrumentality of; denoting an intermediary and not original authorship), *are* all *things, and we are through him.*" (See 1 Corinthians 8:6.)

This does not nullify the fact that Jesus was also created. The term "only-begotten" implies that Jesus was the only being directly created by Yahweh, and all other creations were made "through" him, the only-begotten son. This is emphasized by Paul in his letter to the Colossians:

> . . . giving thanks to the Father, who made us fit to be partakers of the inheritance of the saints in light; who delivered us out of the power of darkness, and translated us into the *Kingdom of the Son* of his love; in whom we have our redemption, the forgiveness of our sins; who is the image of the invisible God, *the*

> *firstborn of all creation.* For by him all things were created, in the heavens and on the earth, things visible and things invisible, whether thrones or dominions or principalities or powers; *all things have been created through him, and for him.* He is before all things, and in him all things are held together. He is the head of the body, the assembly, who is the beginning, *the firstborn from the dead*; that *in all things he might have the preeminence. —Colossians 1:12-18 WEB (emphasis mine)*

To be called the "firstborn from the dead," can only be possible if Jesus actually died (lost his life), something only possible for a created being, since God cannot die.

> For Yahweh will judge his people, and have compassion on his servants . . . "See now that I myself (Yahweh) am he. . . There is no one who can deliver out of my hand. For I lift up my hand to heaven and declare, *as I live forever.*" *—Deuteronomy 32:36,39,40 WEB (emphasis mine)*

> A prayer of Moses, the man of God. O Lord, *you have been our help in all generations.* Before the mountains were born and you brought forth the earth and the world, even *from everlasting to everlasting*, you are God. *—Psalm 90:1,2 LEB (emphasis mine)*

> But you, O Yahweh, abide forever. . . Your years continue throughout all generations. . . Long ago you laid the foundation of the earth, and the heavens are the work of your hands. . . They will perish, but you will endure. And like a garment they will all wear out, you will replace them like clothing,

> and they will be set aside. . . . But you are the same, *and your years do not end. —Psalm 102:12, 24-27 LEB (emphasis mine)*

> Since you are in the presence of God, *who gives life to everything,* and in the presence of the Messiah Jesus, who gave a good testimony before Pontius Pilate, I solemnly charge you to keep these commands stainlessly and blamelessly until the appearance of our Lord Jesus, the Messiah. At the right time, he [Yahweh] will make him [Jesus] known. God [Yahweh] is the blessed and only Ruler, the King of kings and Lord of lords. *He alone has endless life and lives in inaccessible light. No one has ever seen him, nor can anyone see him.* Honor and eternal power belong to him! Amen. *—1 Timothy 6:13-16 ISV (emphasis mine).*

1 Timothy 6 leads us into John 1:18, as John wrote a statement similar to Paul.

> **John 1:18:** *No one has seen God at any time.* The one and only Son, who is in the bosom of the Father, he has declared him. *—WEB*

Many people saw Jesus. John saw Jesus. He said in verse 14 that Jesus (the Word) became flesh. Yet no one has seen God, just as Paul had written to Timothy, "No one has ever seen him, nor can anyone see him."

The oldest manuscripts of John say "only-begotten god" (μονογενὴς θεὸς, mŏnŏgĕnās thĕ-ŏs) at John 1:18, and the context preceding verse 18 supports a literal translation. Jesus was the "only-begotten god." Yahweh, the Creator, created Jesus as the first "son of god," who he used to create all other heavenly beings (*elohim*), and everything else in our universe. While others living in the spiritual realm and men on earth can be called “gods,” they were not begotten directly by the Creator. (See Colossians 1:12-18.)

> **John 3:16,17:** For God so loved the world, that he gave his one and only Son, that whoever believes in him should not perish, but have eternal life. For God didn’t send his Son into the world to judge the world, but that the world should be saved through him. —*WEB*

Did God come to Earth or did God send his son? Jesus was begotten, born, or created as a child from a father, and he was transferred (sent) by his father to be born from Mary’s womb as the promised Messiah.

> **John 5:26:** “For as the Father has life in himself, even so he gave to the Son also to have life in himself.” —*WEB*

John quotes Jesus in this verse, who says the Father “gave” to his son life. Other translations say the Father “granted” the son to have life (ESV, LEB, NET, TCENT, ISV, WNT). Both “gave” and “grant” are perfectly acceptable translations, because they both indicate without Yahweh’s action Jesus would not be alive. Jesus recognizes the life he has is due to his Father. The Greek verb here is ἔδωκεν, ĕdōkĕn (he gives), the aroist, active, indicative, third-person, singular of δίδωμι, *dĭdōmi* (to give, grant). The reality that everything Jesus has was given to him is reflected in other statements recorded in John’s Gospel.

> At John 6:57 Jesus says, “I live because of the Father.” —*LEB*

> John the Baptist said, "The Father loves the Son, and has given all things into his hand," *—John 3:35 WEB*

> Jesus said these things, and lifting up his eyes to heaven, he said, "Father, the time has come. Glorify your Son, that your Son may also glorify you; *even as you gave him authority over all flesh*, so he will give eternal life *to all whom you have given him. . .* I glorified you on the earth. *I have accomplished the work which you have given me to do." —John 17:1,4 WEB (emphasis mine)*

> "Father, I desire that they also *whom you have given me* be with me where I am, that they may see my glory, *which you have given me*, for you loved me before the foundation of the world.*" —John 17: 24 WEB (emphasis mine)*

Along with acknowledging everything was given to him by his father, Jesus also makes this very direct statement:

> "This is eternal life, that they should know you, the only true God, and him whom you sent, Jesus Christ." *—John 17:3 LEB*

The only true God to Jesus is his Father.

> **John 5:27:** "He [Yahweh] also gave him [Jesus] authority to execute judgment, because he is a son of man. " —WEB

This statement may seem to contradict the statement at John 3:17 that says, "For God didn't send his Son into the world to judge the world" (WEB). We must look at the context of each verse to discern why John would have written two apparently opposing statements.

At John 3:16,17 the main point is that Yahweh sent his only son into the world to make eternal life possible for Adam's dying offspring. Judgment is not the focus during this stage of Jesus mission for God. God's will at this point is for Jesus to willingly give his perfect human life as a sacrifice; the price necessary to buy back what Adam lost for his progeny. (See Matthew 20:28; 1 Corinthians 6:19,20.)

> Not to judge, or pronounce sentence on mankind. God might justly have sent him for this. Man deserved condemnation, and it would have been right to have pronounced it; but God was willing that there should be an offer of pardon, and the sentence of condemnation was delayed. But, although Jesus did not come then to condemn mankind, yet the time is coming when he will return to judge the living and the dead, Act 17:31; 2Co 5:10; Mat 25:31-46. *Barnes, Albert, Notes on the Bible, 1847-1885, John 3:17.*

At John 5:27 the focus is what God has given Jesus—life, and the authority to judge. The context here is the resurrection of the dead and what will happen once that occurs.

> Most certainly, I tell you, the hour comes, and now is, when the dead will hear the Son of God's voice; and those who hear will live. For as the Father has life in himself, even so he gave to the Son also to have life in himself. He also gave him authority to execute judgment, because he is a son of man. Don't marvel at this, for the hour comes, in which all that are in the tombs will hear his voice, and will

> come out; those who have done good, to the resurrection of life; and those who have done evil, to the resurrection of judgment. —*John 5: 25-29 LEB*

> **Hath given him authority** - Hath appointed him to do this. Has made him to be judge of all. This is represented as being the appointment of the Father, Act 17:31. The word "authority" here (commonly rendered "power") implies all that is necessary to execute judgment - all the physical power to raise the dead, and to investigate the actions and thoughts of the life; and all the "moral right" or authority to sit in judgment on the creatures of God. *Barnes, Albert, Notes on the Bible, 1847-1885, John 5: 27.*

> **John 5:30:** "I can of myself do nothing. As I hear, I judge, and my judgment is righteous; because I don't seek my own will, but the will of my Father who sent me." —*WEB*

Jesus submits to the will of his Father, who sent him. He is on a mission for God so does nothing on his own initiative but is guided by his Father's will.

> **John 8:58:** Jesus said to them, "Truly, truly I say to you, before Abraham was, I am!" —*LEB*

This last scripture from John is among the most misunderstood verses in the gospel, because of the way it is explained by believers in the Triune Godhead. They insist the "I am" statement by Jesus is a direct reference to Exodus 3:14, thus proclaiming Jesus is God Almighty. This view is supported by translations that read like the King James Version:

> And God said unto Moses, I AM that I AM: and he said, Thus shalt thou say unto the children of Israel, I AM hath sent me unto you. —*Exodus 3:14 KJV*

Did the Jews refer to their God as the I AM? No. They called him by his proper name, Yahweh (6,720 times in the LEB).

The KJV "I AM that I AM" is not the best translation of the Hebrew אהיה אשר אהיה (*ehaye asher ehaye*). אהיה (*ehaye*) is the first-person imperfect form of the verb היה (*hâyâh*), defined as: to exist, that is, be or become, come to pass (see *Strong's Hebrew and Greek Dictionaries* from *Strong's Concordance, 1890*, and *Brown-Driver-Briggs, Hebrew Definitions, 1906*). The meaning is better expressed by these other translations:

> "I will be what I will be," —*ANTB*
>
> "I will become whatever I please," —*TEB*
>
> "I will be what I will be," —*BLE*

These translations don't present the expression *ehaye* as a title, because they are translating the meaning of the entire phrase. In this short statement, Yahweh tells Moses he will be what he will be; his nature, his personality, will be revealed to his chosen people over time. He is not establishing a new title for himself. In the next verse He tells Moses what to call him:

> And God said again to Moses, "So you must say to the Israelites, '*Yahweh*, the God of your ancestors, the God of Abraham, the God of Isaac, and the God of Jacob, has sent me to you. *This is my name forever, and this is my remembrance from generation to generation.'"* —*Exodus 3:15 LEB (emphasis mine)*

The name Yahweh is derived from the verb היה, *hâyâh* (to be, to exist), and denotes simply "the existing one," which is why Yahweh used the phrase *ehaye asher ehaye,* which expresses the underlying aspect of his proper name: the one who *will be what he will be.*

While it is true the Septuagint has the phrase ἐγὼ εἰμί (ĕgō eimi), in the Greek translation of Exodus 3:14, it is not the same as what John wrote at John 8:58.

> Exodus 3:14: ἐγὼ εἰμί ὁ ὤν, (ĕgō eimi hŏ ōn). —*LXX*

> John 8:58: ἐγὼ εἰμί, (ĕgō eimi). —*TGNT*

Notice how the following English versions of the Septuagint translate ĕgō eimi hŏ ōn:

> "I am THE BEING." —*BES*
>
> "I am The One Who Is." —*NETS*

These English translations emphasize God's existence; similar to what is said in the Hebrew. This is made apparent in the next clause of this verse.

> "Thus shall ye say to the children of Israel, THE BEING has sent me to you." —*BES*

> "Thus shall you say to the sons of Israel, 'The One Who Is has sent me to you.'" —*NETS*

These translations do not use the "I am" phrase of other translations in this clause. They correctly repeat what is said in the previous clause, because that is the purpose of the statement. The Israelites were slaves in Egypt where multiple gods were worshiped, and their experience with Yahweh was just beginning. The statement in Exodus 3:14 directs our focus to the existence of Yahweh; the only god who will prove to be what he will be, the existing one, the God who is above every other god.

If John wanted to connect the words of Jesus to the Greek Septuagint, he would have said ἐγὼ εἰμί ὁ ὢν, (ĕgō eimi hŏ ōn). If John wanted to match Jesus' words to the Hebrew scriptures, he could have written the Hebrew words, similar to Matthew's use of the Aramaic words recorded at Matthew 27:46.

So what is the meaning of Jesus' statement at John 8:58?

Notice how *The Modern New Testament* translates the verse from Aramaic sources:

> "I say to you, Before Abraham was born, I was."
> —*TMNT*

Other translations from the Greek:

> "I existed before Abraham was born!" —*AAT*
>
> "I existed before Abraham was born," —*CPV*
>
> "I existed before Abraham was born," —*ONT.*
>
> "I was in existence before Abraham was ever born,"
> —*TLB.*
>
> "Before Abraham existed, I was," —*20CNT.*
>
> "I existed before Abraham was born," —*WNT.*

Why do these NT translations focus on "existence" and not the supposed title, "I Am?" Because the question from the Jews was not, "Who are you?" The question was, "You are not yet fifty years old, and have you seen Abraham?"

The Greek word εἰμί (eimi) can be defined multiple ways:

> εἰμί: to be, to exist, to happen, to be present. Part of Speech: verb. *Thayer's Greek-English Lexicon of the New Testament, Thayer, Joseph, 1896, Fourth Edition, T&T Clark, Fourteenth Printing, 2019, Hendrickson Publishers.*

The expression *ĕgō eimi* is often translated as a perfect indicative verb phrase, which means the action started in the past and is continuing into the present. While it may be in the present tense when isolated, the context will determine the actual tense of the phrase, which is common in Ancient Greek. Examples where present tense verbs are used in past context: Luke 2:48; 13:7; John 5:6; 14:9; Acts 15:21;1 John 3:8.

Based on the original context, there is no indication the Greek statement, *ĕgō eimi*, at Exodus 3:14 and John 8:58, was meant as a title for Yahweh or his Messiah. "I am" is an expression of the verb "to be" and is used by everyone to identify themselves. This is the case at both Exodus 3:14 and John 8:58, and should be rendered contextually as a response to the questions asked. Those claiming the phrase to be a title are turning the verb phrase into a noun, which is out of context and a grammatical error.

Jesus' statement about his existence before Abraham was born agrees with the proclamation by the prophet Micah:

> As for you, Bethlehem Ephrathah, seemingly insignificant among the clans of Judah—from you a king will emerge who will rule over Israel on my [Yahweh's] behalf, *one whose origins*[6] *are in the distant past. —Micah 5:2 NET (emphasis mine)*

Jesus had a pre-human origin that preceded the birth of Abraham. As an *elohim*, a heavenly being, he witnessed the creation of our universe, the creation of the Earth, and the creation of Adam. (See John 1:1 and John 1:14 above). He was sent by Yahweh to be the Messiah and was born a human being to fulfill his Father's will. (See John 3:16, 17).

---

6. Jesus had an origin, a beginning. Yahweh has no origin. Yahweh has always existed. "Before time was, and for ever, you are God," (Psalm 90:2 BBE). The NET says, "The eternal God."

Chapter 12

Jesus in Acts

> **Acts 1:7:** But he said to them, "It is not for you to know the times or seasons that the Father has set by his own authority." —*LEB*

Only the Father has jurisdiction over times and seasons. The Father is in charge, not Jesus. The same verse as translated in the Contemporary English Version:

> Jesus said to them, "You don't need to know the time of those events *that only the Father controls.*" —*CEV (emphasis mine)*

> **Acts 2:22:** Israelite men, listen to these words! Jesus the Nazarene, a man attested to you by God with deeds of power and wonders and signs that *God did through him* in your midst, just as you yourselves know. —*LEB* (*emphasis mine*)

Peter is speaking in this verse and he says God did deeds of power and wonders *through* Jesus. Many Prophets in the past (Elijah, Elisha, and others), and many prophets after them (all the apostles and other anointed Christians), performed deeds of power and wonders, but not of their own accord; their deeds were done by God through them, just like Jesus.

> **Acts 2:32,33:** This Jesus God raised up, of which we all are witnesses. Therefore, having been exalted to the right hand of God and having received the promise of the Holy Spirit from the Father, he has poured out this that you see and hear. —*LEB*

God resurrected Jesus. Jesus was exalted to the right hand of God and given holy spirit as a reward for his faithfulness to God. The gift of holy spirit was then given by Jesus to the faithful Christians on the day of Pentecost, 50 days after his Passover resurrection.

> **Acts 5:30, 31:** The God of our fathers raised up Jesus, whom you killed by hanging him on a tree. This one God has exalted to his right hand as Leader and Savior to grant repentance to Israel and forgiveness of sins. —*LEB*

The "God of our fathers" is Yahweh, the God of Abraham, Isaac, and Jacob. Yahweh resurrected Jesus. Peter then says that God gave Jesus his position as Leader and Savior. This is the main theme throughout Acts. Over and over again Jesus is the one raised up from death by God, who was exalted to God's right hand, given holy spirit to anoint faithful Christians, and one day will deliver judgment and grant repentance to Israel and forgiveness of sins. Jesus is never identified as God Almighty. He is the Son of Man, the Messiah, the Lord who gave his life for all of Adam's offspring.

Saviors raised up by Yahweh are mentioned elsewhere in scripture:

> When the children of Israel cried to Yahweh, Yahweh raised up a savior to the children of Israel, who saved them, even Othniel the son of Kenaz, Caleb's younger brother. *—Judges 3:9 WEB*

> But when the children of Israel cried to Yahweh, Yahweh raised up a savior for them, Ehud the son of Gera, the Benjamite, a left-handed man. *—Judges 3:15 WEB*

> Yahweh gave Israel a savior, so that they went out from under the hand of the Syrians; and the children of Israel lived in their tents as before. *—2 Kings 13:5 WEB*

> It will be for a sign and for a witness to Yahweh of Armies in the land of Egypt; for they will cry to Yahweh because of oppressors, and he will send them a savior and a defender, and he will deliver them. *—Isaiah 19:20 WEB*

Jesus is the ultimate Savior who's sacrifice will have everlasting effects for those who believe in him.

> **Acts 10:38:** Jesus of Nazareth—how *God anointed him with the Holy Spirit and with power*, who went about doing good and healing all who were oppressed by the devil, *because God was with him.* *—LEB* (*emphasis mine*)

Peter again explains how Jesus was able to accomplish his miracles; he was anointed by God *with holy spirit and with power.* (see Acts 2:22). Without this anointing the healing of those oppressed by the devil would not have happened. God was with him, just as God was with other prophets who performed miracles.

(See 1 Kings 17:10-24; 2 Kings 2:8,19-22; 2 Kings 4:1-7, 38-44; Acts 3:1-10; Acts 5:12-16; Acts 6:8; Acts 8:6-13; Acts 9:40; Acts 14:9,10; Acts 19:11,12; Acts 20:7-12.)

Chapter 13

Jesus in Paul's Letters

To the Romans

> **Romans 1:3,4** Regarding his Son. He was a descendant of David with respect to his humanity and was declared by the resurrection from the dead to be the powerful Son of God according to the spirit of holiness—Jesus the Messiah, our Lord. —*ISV*

Here in his introduction, Paul identifies Jesus as the Son of God, the resurrected Messiah, our Lord.

> **Romans 3:24,25** But God treats us much better than we deserve, and because of Christ Jesus, he freely accepts us and sets us free from our sins. God sent Christ to be our sacrifice. Christ offered his life's blood, so that by faith in him we could come to God. And God did this to show that in the past he was right to be patient and forgive sinners. This also shows that God is right when he accepts people who have faith in Jesus. —*CEV*

God sent Jesus to be a sacrifice to set Adam's offspring free from sin. If we have faith in his sacrifice we can be adopted from Adam's imperfect dying family into God's living family.

> **Romans 6:9** Knowing that Christ, because he has been raised from the dead, is going to die no more, death no longer being master over him. —*LEB*

Jesus died and was resurrected by God, no longer susceptible to death as a reward for his faithfulness. Jesus exchanged the value of his perfect human life for the life that Adam lost, willingly forsaking his potential to produce a perfect race of humans, so that Adam's imperfect offspring could choose for themselves to honor God and live forever, without the inherited condemnation passed on from Adam. (See 1 Corinthians 7:23; 1 Peter 1:18,19.)

> **Romans 8:11-17** But if the Spirit of him who made Jesus come again from the dead is in you, he who made Christ Jesus come again from the dead will in the same way, through his Spirit which is in you, give life to your bodies which now are under the power of death. So then, my brothers, we are in debt, not to the flesh to be living in the way of the flesh: For if you go in the way of the flesh, death will come on you; but if by the Spirit you put to death the works of the body, you will have life. And all those who are guided by the Spirit of God are sons of God. For you did not get the spirit of servants again to put you in fear, but the spirit of sons was given to you, by which we say, Abba, Father. The Spirit is witness with our spirit that we are children of God: And if we are children, we have a right to a part in the heritage; a part in the things of God, together with Christ; so that if we have a part in his pain, we will in the same way have a part in his glory. —*BBE*

The spirit of God, who raised up Jesus from the dead, will live in us and make our mortal bodies alive. Because of this, we are obligated to no longer live according to the flesh, but to follow Christ's footsteps and live by the spirit within us. All who are led by the spirit are sons of God, having received the spirit of adoption, which makes us joint heirs with Christ, if we prove our faithfulness to God as he did.

Since Jesus was an "heir," who proved his faithfulness to God, he was never equal to Yahweh; an "heir" is not the owner of a thing, he is the receiver of a thing given to him by the original owner, (in this case, Yahweh, the Almighty God).

> **Romans 10:9** That if you confess with your mouth "Jesus is Lord" and believe in your heart that God raised him from the dead, you will be saved. —*LEB*

Paul declares we should confess that Jesus is our "Lord" and believe that God raised him from the dead. This view is consistent: Jesus is not the Almighty God. God (Yahweh) raised Jesus from the dead. There can be no other explanation because death in the bible is a place of inactivity; The absence of life. Once dead, Jesus could do nothing. (See Psalm 146:3,4; Ecclesiastes 9:5,10.)

> **Romans 15:6** So that with one mind you may glorify with one mouth the God and Father of our Lord Jesus Christ. —*LEB*

Paul wrote this statement long after Jesus had ascended into heaven and was seated at the right hand of God, and he declares we should glorify the God and Father of Jesus. So although Jesus was currently in an exalted position in heaven, he still had a God (Yahweh) who was superior to him; no one is mightier than Yahweh, not even Jesus.

To the Corinthians

> **1 Corinthians 1:3,4** Grace to you and peace from God our Father and the Lord Jesus Christ. I give thanks to my God always concerning you, because of the grace of God which was given to you in Christ Jesus. —*LEB*

Paul states clearly that God is "our Father" and Jesus is "the Lord." He thanks "my God" (the Father) for the Corinthian church because of the mercy bestowed upon them via Jesus, the Messiah, "our Lord."

Regarding Jesus, Mathew Henry's *Commentary on the Whole Bible*, says regarding 1 Corinthians 1:4, and the grace given through Christ Jesus:

> "He (Jesus) is the great procurer and disposer of the favours of God. Those who are united to him by faith, and made to partake of his Spirit and merits, are the objects of divine favour. God loves them, bears them hearty good-will, and bestows on them his fatherly smiles and blessings."

All blessings to the faithful come to them through Jesus, the Messiah. This leads us into verse 9:

> **1 Corinthians 1:9** God is faithful, by whom you were called to fellowship with his Son Jesus Christ our Lord. —*LEB*

God is faithful, which means he is true, constant, and will keep his promises.

> He will not deceive. He will not promise, and then fail to perform; he will not commence anything which he

> will not perfect and finish. The object of Paul in introducing the idea of the faithfulness of God here, is to show the reason for believing that the Christians at Corinth would be kept unto everlasting life. The evidence that they will persevere depends on the fidelity of God; and the argument of the apostle is, that as they had been called by Him into the fellowship of his Son, his faithfulness of character would render it certain that they would be kept to eternal life. . . God is faithful to his Son; and will be faithful to all who are united to him. The argument for the perseverance of the saints is, therefore, sure. *Barnes, Albert, Notes on the Bible, 1847-1885, 1 Corinthians 1:9.*

> **1 Corinthians 3:23** And you belong to Christ, and Christ belongs to God. *—NET*

We belong to Christ in the same way Christ belongs to God. Christ follows God's lead, and we follow Christ's lead: we do what Jesus tells us to do, just as Jesus does what God tells him to do. (Compare John 5:19, 30; 1 Corinthians 11:3.)

> **1 Corinthians 6:14** Now God indeed raised the Lord and he will raise us by his power. *—NET*

Just as our resurrection from death depends on God, Jesus' resurrection also depended on God.

> **1 Corinthians 8:6** yet to us there is one God, the Father, from whom are all things, and we are for him, and there is one Lord, Jesus Christ, through whom are all things, and we are through him. *—LEB*

We can explain this verse with an illustration about the

difference between the owner of a company, a manager in that same company and their relationship to the employees. An employee may refer to the manager as his "boss," but that does not usurp the authority of the owner, who can override any decision made by the manager. God [Yahweh] is the owner of the Christian congregation, and Jesus was made Manager (Lord) of the congregation by God [Yahweh]. We can only come to Yahweh through Jesus; we need Jesus' approval because he is the head [Lord] of the congregation. (Compare John 14:6; 1 Corinthians 11:3.)

> **1 Corinthians 15:21,22** For as by a man came death, by a man has come also the resurrection of the dead. For as in Adam all die, so also in Christ shall all be made alive. —*ESV*

The first man Adam was perfect, until he rejected God's authority and willfully sided with Satan in rebellion. The decision to abandoned his creator placed Adam on the path toward his eventual death. Jesus, also a perfect man, maintained his integrity to God under severe circumstances that led to his death. Jesus' faithful adherence to God's will proved a perfect man could withstand the overwhelming pressure to succumb to selfish desire, even if death was the result. His reward was a resurrection to life everlasting. This act of selflessness was the price paid for Adam's rebellion. One perfect life in exchange for what Adam lost; a sacrifice of not just one man, but the potential within that man to father a perfect race of humans, which gives Adam's offspring hope for an eternal future.

> You were bought with a price [*you were actually purchased* with the precious blood of Jesus and made His own]." —*1 Corinthians 6:20 AMP (emphasis mine)*

> **1 Corinthians 15:24-28** Then the end will come; Christ will overcome all spiritual rulers, authorities, and powers, and will hand over the Kingdom to God the Father. For Christ must rule until God defeats all enemies and puts them under his feet. The last enemy to be defeated will be death. For the scripture says, "God put *all* things under his feet." It is clear, of course, that the words "all things" do not include God himself, who puts all things under Christ. But when all things have been placed under Christ's rule, then he himself, the Son, will place himself under God, who placed all things under him; and God will rule completely over all. —*GNB*

Here we see the limitation upon Christ's Kingdom. His rule will end when all enemies are defeated, then Jesus will "hand over the Kingdom to God the Father." There will no longer be a need for Jesus to be a mediator between God and men.

> "The word "end" (τέλος, tĕlŏs) denotes properly a limit, termination, completion of anything. The proper and obvious meaning of the word here is, that then shall be the end or completion of the work of redemption. That shall have been done which was intended to be done by the incarnation and the work of the atonement; the race shall be redeemed; the friends of God shall be completely recovered; and the administration of the affairs of the universe shall be conducted as they were before the incarnation of the Redeemer." *Barnes, Albert, Notes on the Bible, 1847-1885, 1 Corinthians 15:24.*

> "Seeming at variance with Daniel 7:14, "His dominion is an *everlasting* dominion which *shall not pass away*." Really, His [Jesus] giving up of the

> *mediatorial* kingdom to the Father, when the end for which the mediatorial economy was established has been accomplished, is altogether in harmony with its continuing everlastingly. The change which shall then take place, shall be in the *manner* of administration, not in the *kingdom* itself; God shall then come into *direct* connection with the earth, instead of mediatorially, when Christ shall have fully and finally removed everything that severs asunder the holy God and a sinful earth (Colossians 1:20)." *Jamieson, Fausset and Brown, Commentary Critical and Explanatory on the Whole Bible, 1871, 1 Corinthians 15:28.*

> **1 Corinthians 15:45-49** Thus it is written, "The first man Adam became a living being;" the last Adam became a life-giving spirit. But it is not the spiritual that is first but the natural, and then the spiritual. The first man was from the earth, a man of dust; the second man is from heaven. As was the man of dust, so also are those who are of the dust, and as is the man of heaven, so also are those who are of heaven. Just as we have borne the image of the man of dust, we shall also bear the image of the man of heaven. — *ESV*

Here again Paul compares Jesus to Adam. Both perfect men, although with different origins, yet both were confronted by rebellious influences. Adam was unable to resist the temptations and died. Jesus ignored the temptations and became a life-giving spirit. (Compare Hebrews 5:8.)

> **2 Corinthians 1:2,3** Grace to you and peace from God our Father and the Lord Jesus Christ. Blessed is the

> God and Father of our Lord Jesus Christ, the Father of mercies and God of all comfort. —*ESV*

Paul once again in his introduction states the distinction between Jesus and God the Father. The Father is the God of our Lord Jesus Christ, they are not equals. (See also 2 Corinthians 11:31.)

To the Galatians

> **Galatians 1:1** Paul, an apostle (not commissioned and sent from men nor through the agency of man, but through Jesus Christ—the Messiah—and God the Father, who raised Him from the dead). —*AMP*

Paul distinguishes between God the Father and Jesus, the Messiah, who was raised from the dead by God. Jesus did not resurrect himself.

> **Galatians 1:3-5** Grace to you and peace from God the Father and our Lord Jesus Christ, who gave himself for our sins in order to rescue us from the present evil age, according to the will of our God and Father, to whom be the glory forever and ever. Amen. —*LEB*

Again noting the difference between God the Father and our Lord Jesus Christ, Paul emphasizes Jesus sacrifice was done according to God's will, and therefore all glory goes to the Father. (Compare Mark 14:36; Luke 22:42; John 6:38.)

> **Galatians 3:26** For you are all sons of God through faith in Christ Jesus. —*LEB*

Being a son of God does not make that person God, or equal to God, it makes them a son. God has many sons, one only-begotten son, and many sons adopted through faith.

> **Galatians 4:4** But when the fullness of time had come, God sent forth his Son. —*ESV*

Jesus is God's son. There are no verses in Galatians that say Jesus is God. Paul's understanding regarding Jesus is consistent throughout this letter and in complete harmony with his other writings.

To the Ephesians

> **Ephesians 1:2,3** Grace to you and peace from God our Father and the Lord Jesus Christ. Blessed is the God and Father of our Lord Jesus Christ. —*LEB*

Paul continues to begin his letters by identifying God the Father, and our Lord, Jesus Christ, along with offering praise to our Father, the God of Jesus Christ.

> **Ephesians 1:15-20** Because of this I also, hearing of your faith in the Lord Jesus and your love for all the saints, do not cease giving thanks for you, making mention in my prayers, that the God of our Lord Jesus Christ, the glorious Father, may give you a spirit of wisdom and revelation in the knowledge of him (the eyes of your hearts having been enlightened), so that you may know what is the hope of his calling, what are the riches of the glory of his inheritance among the saints, and what is the surpassing greatness of his power toward us who believe, according to the working of his mighty strength which he has worked in Christ, raising him from the dead and seating him at his right hand in the heavenly places. —*LEB*

Here Paul wishes for God, the glorious Father, to give all the disciples a spirit of wisdom and revelation to understand the hope of the inheritance among the faithful that He accomplished in Christ, by raising Jesus from the dead and seating him at His right hand. Jesus is the benchmark of faith, the first man worthy of a resurrection to life everlasting, exalted by God and seated at God's right hand; the model for us to follow.

> **Ephesians 5:1,2** Therefore become imitators of God, as beloved children, and live in love, just as also Christ loved us, and gave himself for us an offering and sacrifice to God for a fragrant smell. —*LEB*

We are to imitate Christ who sacrificed himself to God out of love for God and love for us. Are we willing to die for God as Jesus did?

> **Ephesians 5:19,20** When you meet together, sing psalms, hymns, and spiritual songs, as you praise the Lord with all your heart. Always use the name of our Lord Jesus Christ to thank God the Father for everything. —*CEV*

We are to pray in Jesus' name but not to Jesus. We are to pray to his Father (See Matthew 6:9). God the Father (Yahweh) is the hearer of prayer, and Jesus is the mediator between God and Men (See 1 Timothy 2:5), so always use the name of our Lord Jesus Christ when speaking to God.

To the Philippians

> **Philippians 1:2** May grace and peace from God our Father and the Lord Jesus, the Messiah, be yours! —*ISV*

Again Paul sets apart Jesus and God in his introduction. If Jesus was God, then all he would have had to say was "from God," and that would have been enough. To Paul, God is the Father, Jesus is the Messiah (our Anointed Lord).

> **Philippians 2:5,6** Think this in yourselves which was also in Christ Jesus, who, existing in the form of God, did not consider being equal with God something to be grasped. —*LEB*

This is another scripture that is often corrupted in some translations to fit the Modern Christian belief that implies Jesus had equality with God, but strains the Greek meaning to do so. Example of a twisted translation of Philippians 2:5,6:

> And think the same way that Christ Jesus thought: Christ was truly God. But he did not try to remain equal with God. —*CEV*

When we follow the context of what Paul wrote his intent is much different than what the CEV implies. Paul is writing about the attitude Jesus had before becoming human. Jesus was in the "form" of God, (μορφῇ - morphay: shape; *figuratively* nature: - form), which fits the biblical understanding that all who dwell in the spirit world are *elohim.* Although having a spiritual body in his pre-human existence, Jesus did not act like Satan and try to make himself equal to God. He did not "grasp" at equality with God. The Greek word often translated "grasp" in the text is ἁρπαγμὸν, harpagmŏn: the accusative, singular, masculine form of the root ἁρπάζω, harpadzō, which means: to *seize* (in various applications): - catch (away, up), pluck, pull, take by force. (See *Dictionaries of Hebrew and Greek Words taken from Strong's Exhaustive Concordance, Strong, James,* 1890, G726; *Thayer's Greek-English Lexicon of the New Testament, Thayer, Joseph, 1896, Fourth Edition, T&T Clark, Fourteenth Printing, 2019, Hendrickson Publishers,* G726; *A Pocket Lexicon to the Greek New Testament, Souter, Alexander, Oxford: Clarendon Press, 1917, page 38).*

The idea that God [Yahweh] could relinquish his immortality and become a creature with a lower nature is not a biblical understanding. Yahweh is incorruptible, immortal, which means he cannot degrade to a lower state of existence.

> And to the King of the ages [Yahweh], the incorruptible, invisible, only wise God, [is] honor and glory through the ages of the ages! Amen. *1 Timothy 1:17 —LSV (see also AMP(Classic), YLT)*

The Greek word translated "incorruptible" in 1 Timothy 1:17 is ἀφθάρτῳ, *aphthartō*, the adjective, singular, dative, masculine form of the root ἄφθαρτος, *aphthartŏs*, which means indestructible, imperishable, incorruptible; hence immortal. (See *Dictionaries of Hebrew and Greek Words taken from Strong's Exhaustive Concordance, Strong, James, G862;* 1890; *Thayer's Greek-English Lexicon of the New Testament, Thayer, Joseph, 1896, Fourth Edition, T&T Clark, Fourteenth Printing, 2019, Hendrickson Publishers,* G862; *A Pocket Lexicon to the Greek New Testament, Souter, Alexander, Oxford: Clarendon Press, 1917, page 44.)*

No where in original scripture is Jesus said to be incorruptible before his resurrection. If he had been he would not have been able to die. He was granted immortality (incorruptibility) after his resurrection, as will all faithful Christians. Paul talks about this in his first letter to the Corinthians:

> And this I say, brothers, that *flesh and blood are not able to inherit the Kingdom of God, nor does the corruption inherit the incorruption.* Behold, I tell you a secret: we indeed will not all sleep, but we will all be changed; in a moment, in the twinkling of an eye, in the last trumpet, for it will sound, and *the dead will be raised incorruptible, and we will be changed; for it is necessary for this corruptible to put on*

> *incorruption, and this mortal to put on immortality; —1 Corinthians 15:50-53 (emphasis mine)* See also 1 Peter 1:3,4.

> **Philippians 2:8-11** He humbled himself by becoming obedient to the point of death, that is, death on a cross. Therefore also God exalted him and graciously granted him the name above every name, so that at the name of Jesus every knee should bow, of those in heaven and of those on earth and of those under the earth, and every tongue confess that Jesus Christ is Lord, to the glory of God the Father. —*LEB*

Unlike Satan, Jesus humbled himself to the point of death, and was exalted by God to a position higher than he had before. God also granted him the name above every name, so that all should confess that Jesus is Lord, to the "glory of God the Father." Paul defers glory to the Father who alone is God Almighty, who sent his son to be the savior of the world.

To the Colossians

> **Colossians 1:3** We give thanks always to God the Father of our Lord Jesus Christ when we pray for you. —*LEB*

Paul once again distinguishes God from Jesus our Lord so there is no misunderstanding as his letter progresses. God (Yahweh, the God of Abraham, Issac, and Jacob), is the Father of Jesus.

> **Colossians 1:15** Who is the image of the invisible God, the firstborn of all creation. —*ASV*

This verse has prompted great debate among scholars, some of whom have attempted to change the meaning of the term "firstborn" into something different from what Paul intended. This debate was born out of a need to not have Paul imply that Jesus is a created being, due to their belief that Jesus is part of a Triune Godhead, equal with the Father and Holy Ghost.

As we noted previously, the term "Image of God" is used to identify all beings created with attributes that reflect the Creator, Yahweh. A person cannot be the reflection of someone if they are that someone. God does not reflect himself; he is himself, but others can reflect his attributes. Being the image or reflection of someone does not make us that person, we are an imitation. How well a person demonstrates the qualities of who they reflect depends on their inherent abilities.

Jesus is the image of God, just as Adam was the image of God. (See Genesis 5:1.)

Being "firstborn" should be easy to understand as the meaning is contained in the two syllables that make up the word. πρωτότοκος, *prōtŏtŏkŏs* is the word translated "firstborn," and is the combination of the roots πρωτος, prōtŏs (first) and τεκνον, teknŏn (child). Since God refers to the spirits in heaven as his "sons," (See Job 38:7), it is not without precedent that he would have a firstborn son; a spirit son who was the first created being. This is what Paul implies by the term "firstborn of all creation." Jesus is "of creation," which means he exists because of that process, not as the originator of that process.

Micah 5:2 says, referring to the promised Messiah: "As for you, Bethlehem Ephrathah, seemingly insignificant among the clans of Judah—from you a king will emerge who will rule over Israel on my behalf, one whose origins are in the distant past." (NET) Jesus, the Messiah, had an origin, an ancient beginning.

At John 6:57 Jesus says, "I live because of the Father." (LEB) Only God has life in himself. All created beings owe their existence, their life, to God.

Revelation 3:14 says, "These things saith the Amen (Jesus), the faithful and true witness, the beginning of the creation of God."(KJV)

Paul shifts focus to what the "Firstborn of Creation" accomplished:

> **Colossians 1:16,17** Because all things in the heavens and on the earth were created by him, things visible and things invisible, whether thrones or dominions or rulers or powers, all things were created through him and for him, and he himself is before all things, and in him all things are held together. —*LEB*

Note that "all things were created through him and for him." The pre-human Jesus, existing in the spiritual realm with the Father, was brought forth as a master worker, the craftsman mentioned in Proverbs who helped Yahweh create our universe and everything in it.

> **Colossians 1:18** And he is the head of the body, the church: who is the beginning, the firstborn from the dead; that in all things he might have the preeminence. —*KJV*

Here Paul recognizes Jesus as the head of the Christian congregation, and a different type of firstborn; The first human raised from the dead as a spirit son of God. This fits with God's desire for his son to "become first in everything." (See Colossians 1:18 LEB.)

> **Colossians 3:1** Therefore, if you have been raised together with Christ, seek the things above, where Christ is, seated at the right hand of God. —*LEB*

Paul's description of where Christ sits is not only consistent throughout his writings, it is also significant as to Christ's identity. Christ does not sit on God's throne, he sits at God's right hand, a place of prominence expected for an heir, but also a place of lessor importance than the throne of God. God (Yahweh) is in charge, not Jesus.

> **Colossians 3:17** And whatever you do in word or deed, do it all in the name of the Lord Jesus, giving thanks to God the Father through him. —*NET*

The Lord Jesus is our mediator.

> "No one comes to the Father except through me."
> —*John 14:6 NET*

To the Thessalonians

> **1 Thessalonians 1:2, 3** We give thanks to God always concerning all of you, making mention constantly in our prayers, because we remember your work of faith and labor of love and steadfastness of hope in our Lord Jesus Christ in the presence of our God and Father. —*LEB*

Paul's appreciation for fellow Christians is always directed to God, as he praises their hope in our Lord Jesus the Messiah. Paul does not say, "God the Father" in verse 2, just "God." (Literal: τῷ θεῷ - tō théō; the dative, singular form, "to the God", which makes the reference specific.) This reveals how Paul recognizes the supremacy of God (Yahweh), and how Christ's victory over death, while the focus of our hope, is always due to the will of "our God and Father" who sent him; (ἡμῶν τοῦ θεοῦ καὶ πατρὸς, hēmōn tou theou kai patros [genitive singular]: Literal: of our *the God* and Father).

> In the NT the Father is "the God" (GK *ho theos*), and Jesus is "the Son of the God," (*ho hyios tou theou*).

> *McKenzie, S.J., John L., 1965, Dictionary of the Bible, page 317.*

> **1 Thessalonians 3:13** So that your hearts may be established blameless in holiness before our God and Father at the coming of our Lord Jesus with all his saints. —*LEB*

Again, Paul refers to "our God and Father." (ἡμῶν τοῦ θεοῦ καὶ πατρὸς, our *the God* and Father). This eliminates any possible Godhead implications that may accompany the "God the Father" designation by some theologians.

> **2 Thessalonians 1:1, 2** Paul and Silvanus and Timothy, to the church of the Thessalonians in God our Father and the Lord Jesus Christ. Grace to you and peace from God the Father and the Lord Jesus Christ. —*LEB*

Paul returns to the "God the Father" designation, and yet makes it clear "God" is someone other than the Lord Jesus Christ; he does not say "God the Father" and "God the Son."

> **2 Thessalonians 2:16, 17** Now may our Lord Jesus Christ himself and God our Father, who has loved us and given *us* eternal encouragement and good hope by grace, encourage your hearts and strengthen you in every good work and word. —*LEB*

Sometimes translation can muddle the original Greek and make understanding difficult because of the lack of punctuation in the original language. The above quote from the *Lexham English Bible* separates clauses correctly by placing commas where necessary. The second clause only applies to the Father. This may not be obvious to all readers, so the *Bible in Basic English* rearranged the comas for better comprehension.

> Now our Lord Jesus Christ himself, and God our Father who had love for us and has given us eternal comfort and good hope through grace, give you comfort and strength in every good work and word. *—2 Thessalonians 2:16,17 BBE*

Paul's references to Jesus and the Father never combines them into a Godhead, but always separates them into two distinct individuals; the Father who alone is God, and Jesus who is the promised Messiah, sent by God to do God's will (See John 4:34; 6:38; 8:28.)

To Timothy

> **1 Timothy 1:1,2** Paul, an apostle of Christ Jesus according to the command of God our Savior and of Christ Jesus our hope, to Timothy, my true child in the faith. Grace, mercy, and peace from God the Father and Christ Jesus our Lord. *—LEB*

Paul continues keeping the identities of God and Christ distinctive in his introduction. He is an apostle of Christ by the "command of God," who he designates "our Savior," and of Christ Jesus "our hope." This may be confusing since Jesus is said elsewhere to be our "Savior."

> The name Saviour is as applicable to God the Father as to the Lord Jesus Christ, since God is the great Author of salvation. *Barnes, Albert, Notes on the Bible, 1847-1885, 1 Timothy 1:1.*

> **God our Saviour** — The Father (1Ti 2:3; 1Ti 4:10; Luk 1:47; 2Ti 1:9; Tit 1:3; Tit 2:10; Tit 3:4; Jud 1:25). It

> was a Jewish expression in devotion, drawn from the Old Testament (compare Psa 106:21). *Jamieson, Fausset and Brown, Commentary Critical and Explanatory on the Whole Bible, 1871, 1 Timothy 1:1.*

As previously shown in *Jesus in Acts*, there are many saviors mentioned in scripture. (Compare Judges 3:9; Judges 3:15; 2 Kings 13:5; Isaiah 19:20). All these men were sent by God (Yahweh). Without his intervention no salvation would have occurred. Without God sending his only-begotten son, our ultimate salvation would still be wanting.

> In this is love: not that we have loved God, but that he loved us and sent his Son to be the atoning sacrifice for our sins. —*1 John 4:10 NET*

God (Yahweh) is the Great Savior who sent men called saviors, who saved his people on multiple occasions.

> **1 Timothy 2:5** For there is one God and one mediator between God and human beings, the man Christ Jesus. —*LEB*

Remember the word "Christ" is a title, not a proper name. So the final clause of 1 Timothy 2:5 can be translated, "Jesus, the man *anointed* [by God]."

A mediator is someone who works with both sides in a dispute to help them reach agreement; a go-between, arbitrator, negotiator, moderator, facilitator, referee, umpire, intercessor, conciliator.

Paul identifies Jesus as a separate individual who stands between God and human beings to facilitate our salvation. This point is essential to understand the Christ's position in relation to God. If his mediation is to be successful, he must be no part of the dispute, otherwise his judgment would be biased. This demonstrates the wisdom and justice of God. Having been created an *elohim*, Jesus experienced spiritual life with all the heavenly beings and had personal interaction with Yahweh. Being born a human, Jesus experienced life in the corrupt world of Adam's offspring (See Hebrews 4:15). This gives him the perfect background as a mediator between God and humans; he has the experience and has no personal stake in the dispute.

To Titus

> **Titus 1:1-4** Paul, a slave of God and an apostle of Jesus Christ for the faith of the chosen of God and the knowledge of the truth that is according to godliness, in the hope of eternal life which God, who does not lie, promised before eternal ages, but at the proper time has disclosed his message in the proclamation with which I was entrusted according to the command of God our Savior, to Titus, my true child according to a common faith. Grace and peace from God the Father and Christ Jesus our Savior. —*LEB*

This is another letter from Paul to an individual Christian, and ends abruptly without Paul's final greetings and commendations at the end, as is his style in other letters. Because of this, it seems incomplete. Paul structured this letter specifically for Titus to help him with problems in the local Christian Church on Crete. Unique to this letter is the title Savior. which Paul applies to God three times and to the Christ three times.

Using the term for God is based on usage in the OT and identifies the Father (Yahweh) as the source of all salvation. (See 2 Samuel 22:3; Psalm 17:7; Psalm 106:21; Isaiah 43:3,11; Isaiah 45:15, 21; Isaiah 49:26; Isaiah 60:16; Isaiah 63:8; Jeremiah 14:8.

The Christ's identity as Savior is due to his sacrificial death to save Adam's offspring. (See 1 John 4:9-14; 1 Timothy 1:1,2; Acts 13:23; Jude 1:25.)

To Philemon

> **Philemon 3** Grace to you and peace from God our Father and the Lord Jesus Christ. *LEB.*

Paul again refers to God as "our Father," distinguishing between Him and the Lord Jesus Christ. Paul is consistent in his view of Jesus.

Chapter 14

Jesus in the Letter to the Hebrews

The writer of Hebrews does not identify himself by name, and there is no universal agreement among scholars regarding who authored the letter. However, based on the context, the style, and the time of the composition, I favor the Apostle Paul—the thought prints in Hebrews are Paul's. The general accepted date of the letter is before the fall of Jerusalem, around the year 61 C.E., twenty-eight years after the death of Jesus. Written to Jewish Christians in Judea, who had been suffering persecution from the Jewish religious leaders, the letter provides encouragement and answers to the objections they faced.

No mention is made of Jesus being God in the flesh. Jesus is once again understood to be the Savior sent by God.

> **Hebrews 1:1,2** Although God spoke long ago in many parts and in many ways to the fathers by the prophets, in these last days he has spoken to us by a Son, whom he appointed heir of all things, through whom also he made the world. —*LEB*

Paul contrasts Jesus with the prophets of old, who spoke for God at various times and places. These were the last days of the Mosaic Law and the Jewish religious system (in just 9 years the

Holy Temple would be destroyed and with it the religious system mandated by the Mosaic Law). Note also that the Son is appointed "heir" of all things. If Jesus is God he could not be an heir. The owner of a thing does not inherit that thing, he already owns it. The owner gives it to his offspring who he designates an "heir." Paul also reminds his readers the world was made through God's son, which emphasizes Christ's superiority over the prophets.

> **Hebrews 1:3-6** He is the radiance of the glory of God and the exact imprint of his nature, and he upholds the universe by the word of his power. After making purification for sins, he sat down at the right hand of the Majesty on high, having become as much superior to angels as the name he has inherited is more excellent than theirs. For to which of the angels did God ever say, "You are my Son, today I have begotten you"? Or again, "I will be to him a father, and he shall be to me a son"? And again, when he brings the firstborn into the world, he says, "Let all God's angels worship him." —*ESV*

Here Paul sets Jesus apart from the angels. Jesus was made in the image of God, as were the angels (Compare Genesis 1:26; Job 1:6; 38:7; Psalm 89:6; Luke 20:36), yet he inherited a position and name superior to the angels.

> The Son was made greater than the angels, just as the name that God gave him is greater than theirs. (*Hebrews 1:4 GNB*).

He was "begotten" by God, unlike the angels who were created through Jesus (Compare 1 Corinthians 8:6; John 1:3). As the firstborn of God, and heir, Jesus is worthy of being honored by the angels (See 1 Peter 3:21,22.)

The word often translated "worship" in this verse is προσκυνησάτωσαν, pros-koo-neh-sáht-oh-sahn, the aorist, active, imperative, third person, plural of the root προσκυνέω, pros-koo-néh-oh.

> προσκυνέω—From G4314 and probably a derivative of G2965 (meaning to kiss, like a dog licking his master's hand); to fawn or crouch to, that is, (literally or figuratively) prostrate oneself in homage (do reverence to, adore): - worship." *Strong's Hebrew and Greek Dictionary, G43522.*

The intent here is reverence to a king, as Jesus, the firstborn, has been seated at God's right hand, and given a superior position; a kingship to rule over the nations as the Messianic King. (Compare Daniel 7:13,14; Psalm 2:12.)

> "Psa 89:27 (quoted in Heb 1:5), [Jesus] is called "God's first-born, higher than the kings of the earth"; so the antitypical first-begotten, the son of David, is to be worshiped by all inferior lords, such as angels ("gods," Psa 97:7); for He is "King of kings and Lord of lords" (Rev 19:16)." *Jamieson, Fausset and Brown, Commentary Critical and Explanatory on the Whole Bible, 1871, Hebrews 1:6.*

> **Hebrews 1:8, 9** But of the Son he says, "Your throne, O God, is forever and ever, the scepter of uprightness is the scepter of your kingdom. You have loved righteousness and hated wickedness; therefore God, your God, has anointed you with the oil of gladness beyond your companions. —*ESV*

Here Paul quotes Psalm 45:6,7 and applies it to the Messiah, with reference to his position above the angels. Being called θεός, thĕ-ŏs (god) is a direct copy of the Septuagint version of the Psalm, and follows the same usage of the term in Psalm 82, as applied to both the members of the Divine Council (Psalm 82:1,6), and as reference to the Messiah (Psalm 82:8). This follows the Hebrew use of אלהים, *elohim* and other derivations of אל, el (god), for all those who reside in the spirit realm. (See Chapter 1: Understanding God). This is made clear by the quote in verse 9, "because of this God, your God, has anointed you with the olive oil of joy more than your companions." Jesus is again set apart from the angels, his "companions." He has been anointed by Yahweh to a superior position because of his faithfulness. (Compare Psalm 89:26; Isaiah 61:1; John 20:17; Ephesians 1:3.)

> **Hebrews 1:13** But to which of the angels has he ever said, "Sit down at my right hand, until I make your enemies a footstool for your feet." —*LEB*

Paul quotes Psalm 110 in this verse, as in other places in this letter. The reasons are straightforward, as explained by Albert Barnes:

> "Sit on my right hand;" see notes on Heb 1:3. This passage is taken from Psa 110:1, a Psalm that is repeatedly quoted in this Epistle as referring to the Messiah, and the very passage before is applied by the Saviour to himself, in Mat 22:43-44, and by Peter it is applied to him in Act 2:34-35. There can be no doubt, therefore, of its applicability to the Messiah. . . The phrase "to make an enemy a footstool," is borrowed from the custom of ancient warriors who stood on the necks of vanquished kings on the occasion of celebrating a triumph over them as a token of their complete prostration and subjection; see notes on Isa 10:6. The enemies here referred to are the foes of God and of his religion, and

> the meaning is, that the Messiah is to be exalted until all those foes are subdued. Then he will give up the kingdom to the Father; see notes on 1Co 15:24-28. The exaltation of the Redeemer, to which the apostle refers here, is to the mediatorial throne. In this he is exalted far above the angels. His foes are to be subdued to him, but angels are to be employed as mere instruments in that great work." *Barnes, Albert, Notes on the Bible, 1847-1885, Hebrews 1:13.*

> **Hebrews 2:17** Therefore he was obligated to be made like his brothers in all respects, in order that he could become a merciful and faithful high priest in the things relating to God, in order to make atonement for the sins of the people. —*LEB*

To be "made like his brothers in all respects," Jesus had to be completely human. And as the last Adam (See 1 Corinthians 15: 21,22; 45-49), he was the equal to Adam in every respect except obedience; Adam disobeyed, Jesus was faithful and maintained his integrity to God until his death.

> "For he who sanctifies and those who are sanctified all have one source. That is why he is not ashamed to call them brothers, saying, "I will tell of your name to my brothers; in the midst of the congregation, I will sing your praise." And again, "I will put my trust in him." And again, "Behold, I and the children God has given me." Since therefore the children share in flesh and blood, he himself likewise partook of the same things, that through death he might destroy the one who has the power of death, that is, the devil, and deliver all those who through fear of death were subject to lifelong slavery." —*Hebrews 2:10-15 ESV*

The "children God has given" Jesus are Adam's imperfect offspring, who will be made perfect if repentant believers in Christ's sacrifice, and adopted through their faith. This is an aspect of the great redemption many overlook; how Jesus, as a perfect human could have fathered a perfect family of his own, but chose to adopt Adam's imperfect offspring because they did not choose to be imperfect—they inherited what Adam passed on to them: sickness and death. This act of love for us demanded Christ's death; he willingly gave up his perfect human life as the price for what Adam lost. (Compare 1 Corinthians 6:20.)

> **Hebrews 5:5-8** Thus also Christ did not glorify himself to become high priest, but the one who said to him, "You are my Son, today I have begotten you," just as also in another place he says, "You are a priest forever according to the order of Melchizedek," who in the days of his flesh offered up both prayers and supplications, with loud crying and tears, to the one who was able to save him from death, and he was heard as a result of his reverence. Although he was a son, he learned obedience from what he suffered. —*LEB*

Unlike Satan, who sought to exalt himself, Jesus did not seek to glorify himself, and "learned obedience from what he suffered," recognizing the only source for his own salvation was Yahweh, the one who "was able to save him from death."

> **Hebrews 9:24** For Christ did not enter into a sanctuary made by hands, a mere copy of the true one, but into heaven itself, now to appear in the presence of God on our behalf. —*LEB*

Once resurrected, Christ did not ascend to heaven to put on the mantle of God Almighty. The Greek is very specific: Christ entered to appear before God face to face; νῦν ἐμφανισθῆναι τῷ προσώπῳ τοῦ θεοῦ, nyn em-phanis-thén-ai tō pro-sō-pō tou theou, (Literal: *now to appear in front of the face of the God.)*

> πρόσωπον, (a) the human face; often Hebraistically otiose, e.g. πρὸ προσώπον σου practically = πρὸ σοῦ, Mt. 11:10; πρόσωπον πρὸς πρόσωπον (Hebraistic). face to face; (b) hence applied to God, from His having been originally conceived as in human form, presence (cf. Ac. 5:41); (c) appearance, outward aspect (Mt. 16:3), Lk. 12:56, &c.; surface, Lk. 21:35. *Alexander Souter, A Pocket Lexicon to the Greek New Testament (Oxford: Clarendon Press, 1917), 221–222.*

This fits perfectly with the prophecy in Daniel:

> "I continued watching in the visions of the night, and look, with the clouds of heaven one like a son of man was coming, and he came to the Ancient of Days, and was presented before him. And to him was given dominion and glory and kingship that all the peoples, the nations, and languages would serve him; his dominion is a dominion without end that will not cease, and his kingdom is one that will not be destroyed." *—Daniel 7: 13,14 LEB*

> **Hebrews 10:5,6,7** Therefore, when he came into the world, he said, "Sacrifice and offering you did not want, but a body you prepared for me; you did not delight in whole burnt offerings and offerings for sins. Then I said, 'Behold, I have come—in the roll of the book it is written about me—to do your will, O God.'" *—LEB*

Jesus is speaking in this verse and he states he came to do God's will, not his own will.

> **To do thy will, O God** - This expresses the amount of all that the Redeemer came to do. He came to do the will of God:
>
> (1) By perfect obedience to his Law, and,
>
> (2) By making an atonement for sin - becoming "obedient unto death." Php 2:8.
>
> The latter is the principal thought here, for the apostle is showing that sacrifice and offering such as were made under the Law would not put away sin, and that Christ came in contradistinction from them to make a sacrifice that would be efficacious. Everywhere in the Scriptures it is held out as being the "will of God" that such an atonement should be made. There was salvation in no other way, nor was it possible that the race should be saved unless the Redeemer drank that cup of bitter sorrows; see Mat 26:39. We are not to suppose, however, that it was by mere arbitrary will that those sufferings were demanded. *Barnes, Albert, Notes on the Bible, 1847-1885, Hebrews 10:7.*

> **Hebrews 13:20** Now may the God of peace, who brought up from the dead our Lord Jesus, the great shepherd of the sheep, by the blood of the eternal covenant. —*LEB*

In the final section of his letter, Paul writes a short benediction which identifies the God of peace (Yahweh) as the one who resurrected our Lord Jesus from the dead.

The God of peace (*ho theos tēs eirēnēs*). God is the author and giver of peace, a Pauline phrase (6 times) as in 1Th 5:23.

Who brought again from the dead (*ho anagagōn ek nekrōn*). Second aorist active articular participle of *anagō* (cf. Rom 10:7), the only direct mention of the resurrection of Jesus in the Epistle, though implied often (Heb 1:3, etc.).

That great shepherd of the sheep (*ton poimena tōn probatōn ton megan*). This phrase occurs in Isa 63:11 except *ton megan* which the author adds as in Heb 4:14; Heb 10:21. So here, 'the shepherd of the sheep the great one.'

With the blood of the eternal covenant (*en haimati diathēkēs aiōnio*). This language is from Zec 9:11. The language reminds us of Christ's own words in Mar 14:24 (Mat 26:28; Luk 22:20; 1Co 11:25) about 'my blood of the covenant.' *Word Pictures in the New Testament, A.T. Robertson, 1930, Hebrews 13:20.*

Chapter 15

Jesus in the Letter from James

> **James 1:1** James, a slave of God and of the Lord Jesus Christ, to the twelve tribes in the dispersion. Greetings! —*LEB*

James was a son of Mary and Joseph. He knew Jesus as well as any brother would, and he proclaims to be a slave to him in a religious sense, as well as a slave of God (Yahweh). He does not combine the two individuals into one God; James is a slave to both. He separates Yahweh from Jesus by calling Jesus, "Lord," because of the exalted position given to Jesus by Yahweh.

James refers to Jesus by name only one more time at 2:1 and calls him "our glorious Lord."

As the letter continues, James only refers to God (Yahweh):

We should pray to God and ask for wisdom (1:5).

God temps no one and cannot be tempted by evil (1:13), which disqualifies Jesus from being equal to Yahweh, because Jesus was tempted by Satan at every opportunity; The possibility existed that the temptations would be successful, otherwise Satan would not have tried to corrupt Jesus (see Luke 4:1-13).

Human anger does not accomplish the righteousness of God (1:20).

Undefiled religion is determined by God our Father, not Jesus (1:27).

God chooses who will be heirs of the kingdom (2:5). The heirs are the children God has given Jesus. (Compare Hebrews 2:10-15).

God is one, and even the demons believe that and shudder (2:19).

Abraham believed God and was called God's friend (2:23). (Compare Isaiah 41:8; 2 Chronicles 20:7).

Friends of the world are enemies of God (4:4).

God opposes the proud (4:6).

We should subject ourselves to God and oppose the devil (4:7).

If we draw near to God, he will draw near to us (4:8).

Chapter 16

Jesus in Peter's Letters

> **1 Peter 1:3** Blessed be the God and Father of our Lord Jesus Christ, who according to his great mercy has caused us to be born again to a living hope through the resurrection of Jesus Christ from the dead. —*LEB*

Peter, one of the original twelve apostles, knew because of the "great mercy" of God the Father all Christians have hope, because He resurrected Jesus. Peter did not view Jesus as God. He knew the Father was the God of Jesus, the one who brought him back to life.

> **1 Peter 1:18-21** Knowing that you were ransomed from the futile ways inherited from your forefathers, not with perishable things such as silver or gold, but with the precious blood of Christ, like that of a lamb without blemish or spot. He was foreknown before the foundation of the world but was made manifest in the last times for the sake of you, who through him are believers in God, who raised him from the dead and gave him glory, so that your faith and hope are in God. —*ESV*

The ransom of Jesus' perfect life was for our benefit, that we might have "faith and hope" not in Jesus, but in God, who sent his son to be our ransom. God accepts that offering and will apply it to us if we believe He raised Jesus from the dead and gave him glory. That is the gift to us from God, the precious life of his only son, who proved that a perfect man could remain faithful to God, even unto death. Christ's victory is the ransom equal to the life Adam lost.

> **1 Peter 3:18** For Christ also suffered once for sins, the just for the unjust, in order that he could bring you to God, being put to death in the flesh, but made alive in the spirit. —*LEB*

Christ died to bring us to God. We are redeemed by the just life he relinquished; the price paid for our unjust lives.

> **1 Peter 3:21.22** And also, corresponding to this, baptism now saves you, not the removal of dirt from the flesh, but an appeal to God for a good conscience through the resurrection of Jesus Christ, who is at the right hand of God, having gone into heaven, with angels and authorities and powers having been subjected to him. —*LEB*

Peter says baptism is "an appeal to God for a good conscience," through the resurrection of Jesus. To Peter, Jesus is not God. He views Jesus as the means by which God will reconcile humankind to himself. Jesus is at God's right hand, a place of eminent authority, "with angels, authorities, and powers" subjected to him, which is a new position given to him because of his faithfulness to God. (Compare Ephesians 1:20,21)

> The reason why the apostle here adverts to the fact that the Lord Jesus is raised up to the right hand of

> God, and is so honored in heaven, seems to have been to encourage those to whom he wrote to persevere in the service of God, though they were persecuted. The Lord Jesus was in like manner persecuted. He was reviled, and rejected, and put to death. Yet he ultimately triumphed. . . As Noah, who had been faithful and steadfast when surrounded by a scoffing world, was at last preserved by his faith from ruin, and as the Redeemer, though persecuted and put to death, was at last exalted to the right hand of God, so would it be with them if they bore their trials patiently, and did not faint or fail in the persecutions which they endured. *Barnes, Albert, Notes on the Bible, 1847-1885, 1 Peter 3:22.*

> **2 Peter 1:2** May grace and peace be multiplied to you in the knowledge of God and of Jesus our Lord. —*LEB*

Peter's separation of God and Jesus here is significant. Knowledge of both is important, yet Peter does not equate Jesus with God. Peter calls Jesus, "Lord."

> **2 Peter 1:17** For he received honor and glory from God the Father when a voice such as this was brought to him by the Majestic Glory, "This is my beloved Son, in whom I am well pleased." —*LEB*

> **For he received from God the Father honour and glory** - He [Jesus] was honored by God in being thus addressed.

> **When there came such a voice to him from the excellent glory** - The magnificent splendor; the bright cloud which overshadowed them. Mat 17:5.

> **This is my beloved Son, in whom I am well pleased** - See the notes at Mat 17:5; Mat 3:17. This demonstrated that he [Jesus] was the Messiah. Those who heard that voice could not doubt this; they never did afterwards doubt." *Barnes, Albert, Notes on the Bible, 1847-1885, 2 Peter 1:17.*

The words that Peter heard say it plain enough for anyone to understand. Jesus is not God (the Almighty Creator, Yahweh), he is God's son.

Chapter 17

Jesus in John's Letters

> **1 John 1:5-7** And this is the message which we have heard from him and announce to you, that God is light and there is no darkness in him at all. If we say that we have fellowship with him and walk in the darkness, we lie and do not practice the truth. But if we walk in the light as he is in the light, we have fellowship with one another, and the blood of Jesus his Son cleanses us from all sin. —*LEB*

John says, "we do not practice the truth" if we walk in darkness. So removing darkness from our worship is essential to pleasing God. If we walk in light, we have fellowship with God and the blood of Jesus cleanses us from sin. Our worship must be pure and free of all pagan influence, otherwise it is corrupt and unworthy of God's fellowship.

> **1 John 3:8** The one who practices sin is of the devil, because the devil has been sinning from the beginning. For this reason the Son of God was revealed: in order to destroy the works of the devil. —*LEB*

The son of God was revealed to us by the human birth of Jesus. Before that he was *elohim*, unseen in the spirit realm. God sent him to us to not only redeem us from the sin we inherited from Adam, but to destroy everything the devil has done in opposition to Yahweh.

> **1 John 4:9, 10** By this the love of God is revealed in us: that God has sent his one and only Son into the world so that we may live through him. In this is love: not that we have loved God, but that he loved us and sent his Son to be the atoning sacrifice for our sins. —*NET*

John repeats what he wrote in his gospel: God sent his son to be our savior by sacrificing his perfect life for our imperfect lives. Jesus willingly complied with his father's will. (See John 3:16.)

> **1 John 4:12** No one has seen God at any time. If we love one another, God resides in us and his love is perfected in us. —*LEB*

John repeats what he wrote in his gospel: "No one has ever seen God." (See John 1:18.) John knew this was an absolute truth from his understanding of the Torah.

> And Yahweh said to Moses, "Also I will do this thing that you have spoken, because you have found favor in my eyes and I have known you by name." And he [Moses] said, "Please show me your glory." And he [Yahweh] said, "I myself will cause all my goodness to pass over before you, and I will proclaim the name of Yahweh before you, and I will be gracious to whom I will be gracious, and I will show compassion to whom I will show compassion." But he said, "You are not able

> to see my face, because a human will not see me and live." —*Exodus 33: 17-20 LEB*

Since people saw Jesus, Jesus cannot be God. (Compare Hebrews 12:29.)

> **1 John 4:15** Whoever confesses that Jesus is the Son of God, God resides in him and he in God. —*LEB*

Why would John need to say this? He tells us beginning at 1 John 4:2:

> By this you know the Spirit of God: every spirit that confesses Jesus Christ has come in the flesh is from God, and every spirit that does not confess Jesus is not from God, and this is the spirit of the antichrist, of which you have heard that it is coming, and now it is already in the world. You are from God, little children, and have conquered them, because the one who is in you is greater than the one who is in the world. They are from the world; therefore they speak from the world and the world listens to them. We are from God. The one who knows God listens to us; whoever is not from God does not listen to us. By this we know the Spirit of truth and the spirit of deceit. —*1 John 4: 2-6 LEB*

By proclaiming Jesus is God and part of a trinity of gods, Christendom has acquired the spirit of deceit, the spirit of antichrist, by incorporating pagan theology into their approved doctrine. They may confess that Jesus came in the flesh, but they deny his humanity when they proclaim he was God in the flesh, equal to the Father, and not a son of the Most High, the Messiah, born a perfect man and equal to Adam. (Compare Romans 5:14; 1 Corinthians 15:22,45.)

> **1 John 5:5** Now who is the one who conquers the world except the one who believes that Jesus is the Son of God? —*LEB*

John could not be more straightforward in his meaning than he is in this verse: Jesus is the Son of God.

> **1 John 5:9, 10** If we receive the testimony of people, the testimony of God is greater, because this is the testimony of God that he has testified concerning his Son. (The one who believes in the Son of God has the testimony in himself. The one who does not believe God has made him a liar, because he has not believed in the testimony that God has testified concerning his Son.) —*LEB*

There is no scripture that proclaims Yahweh said Jesus is his equal, but there is scripture that proclaims Yahweh said Jesus is his son. (See Matthew 2:15; 3:17; 17:5; Mark 1:11; 9:7; Luke 3:22; 9:35; 2 Peter 1:17.) And there is scripture that quotes Jesus stating his relationship with his father. (See John 5:19; 14:28; 20:17.)

> **1 John 5:11, 12** And this is the testimony: that God has given us eternal life, and this life is in his Son. The one who has the Son has the life; the one who does not have the Son of God does not have the life.
> —*LEB*

Eternal life is given to us by God, who also gave it to his son (See John 5:26). Our salvation comes only through Jesus. Professed Christians who do not have the son of God will not have life. (Compare John 14:6.)

> "Not everyone who says to me, 'Lord, Lord,' will enter into the kingdom of heaven, but the one who does the will of my Father who is in heaven. On that day many will say to me, 'Lord, Lord, did we not prophesy in your name, and expel demons in your name, and perform many miracles in your name?' And then I will say to them plainly, 'I never knew you. Depart from me, you who practice lawlessness!'" — *Matthew 7: 21-23 LEB*

Only Christians call Jesus, "Lord." So the revelation in Matthew's gospel rings true to the state of deceit that would exist within Christendom.

> **1 John 5:13** These things I have written to you who believe in the name of the Son of God, in order that you may know that you have eternal life. —*LEB*

All we can bring to God is our belief. Nothing else will result in salvation. No act, nothing we do in this world will buy our way into heaven. Only the ransom paid by Jesus nullifies our imperfection and allows us to fellowship with God, if we believe and set our hope upon Christ's sacrifice. Our relationship with God must be fueled by a desire to follow Jesus according to truth, and not the lawless tradition that has corrupted the word of God.

> **1 John 5:20** And we know that the Son of God has come and has given us understanding, in order that we may know the one who is true, and we are in the one who is true, in his Son Jesus Christ. This one is the true God and eternal life. —*LEB*

The "one who is true," the "true God," is Yahweh, the Almighty Creator, and the Father of Jesus the Messiah. (See John 17:3.) He is the living one, the one who resurrected Jesus, and the one who can give us eternal life, a life that Adam rejected, and that Jesus made possible by his sacrifice. (See 1 John 5:11; Compare John 5:26; 14:6.)

> **2 John 1:3** Grace, mercy, peace will be with us from God the Father and from Jesus Christ the Son of the Father in truth and love. —*LEB*

In the opening greeting of his second letter, John makes clear the distinction between God and Jesus. God (Yahweh) is the Father, Jesus is the son of the Father. (Ἰησοῦ Χριστοῦ τοῦ υἱοῦ τοῦ πατρός, Iēsou Christou tou uiou tou patrŏs). (Compare Colossians 1:15,18; Romans 8:29; Revelation 1:5; 3:14.)

Chapter 18

Jesus in Jude's Letter

> **Jude 1** Jude, a slave of Jesus Christ, and a brother of James, to those who have been called, who are beloved by God the Father and have been kept through union with Jesus Christ. —*WNT*

Jude does not mention his familial relationship to Jesus (his half-brother through Joseph), but emphasizes his spiritual relationship by referring to himself as a "slave of Jesus" the anointed Messiah. Like the other authors of the Christian letters, Jude separates God the Father from Jesus the Messiah. A Christian's union with Jesus is what ensures salvation. (Compare Acts 4:10-12.)

> **Jude 25** To the only God our Savior, through Jesus Christ our Lord, be glory, majesty, power, and authority before all time and now and for all eternity. Amen.—*LEB*

Jude reminds his readers that our salvation is due to Yahweh, "the only God our Savior," and our everlasting salvation is possible "through Jesus Christ our Lord." (Compare Acts 5:30,31, Judges 3:9,15, 2 Kings 13:5, Isaiah 19:20.)

The “glory, majesty, power, and authority” praise is directed to “the God our Savior,” through Jesus, which is the correct path we must all take when praising God.

> Jesus said to him, “I am the way, the truth, and the life. No one comes to the Father except through me.”
> —*John 14:6 LEB*

Chapter 19

Jesus in John's Revelation

> **Revelation 1:1,2** The revelation of Jesus Christ, which God gave him to show to his slaves the things which must take place in a short time, and communicated it by sending it through his angel to his slave John, who testified about the word of God and the testimony of Jesus Christ, all that he saw. —*LEB*

This book is a revealing about the future that God gave Jesus Christ, which means God (Yahweh) knew things Jesus did not know. (Compare Matthew 24:36; Mark 13:32.) Jesus then sent an angel to deliver the information to John. This reveals the hierarchy of information distribution: Yahweh to Jesus to an Angel to John.

> **Revelation 1:4,5** John, to the seven churches in Asia: grace to you and peace from the one who is and the one who was and the one who is coming, and from the seven spirits who are before his throne, and from Jesus Christ the faithful witness, the firstborn from the dead and the ruler of the kings of the earth.—*LEB*

Greek composition can be difficult to follow, but excellent translations properly separate clauses to define meaning accurately. However, lacking the mindset of a first-century Christian, some terms used may be unfamiliar with modern-day readers. Who is meant by "the one who is and the one who was and the one who is coming?" The *Good News Bible* paraphrases the clause to help us understand:

> Grace and peace be yours from God, who is, who was, and who is to come. —*Revelation 1: 4, GNB*

> **Him which is . . . Was . . . is to come**—a periphrasis for the incommunicable name Jehovah, the self-existing One, unchangeable. In Greek the indeclinability of the designation here implies His unchangeableness. Perhaps the reason why "He which is to come" is used, instead of "He that shall be," is because the grand theme of Revelation is the Lord's coming (Rev 1:7). Still it is THE FATHER as distinguished from "Jesus Christ" (Rev 1:5) who is here meant. But so one are the Father and Son that the designation, "which is to come," more immediately applicable to Christ, is used here of the Father. *Jamieson, Fausset and Brown, Commentary Critical and Explanatory on the Whole Bible, 1871, Revelation 1:4.*

> **From him which is, and which was, and which is to come** — From him who is everlasting — embracing all duration, past, present, and to come. No expression could more strikingly denote eternity than this. He now exists; he has existed in the past; he will exist in the future. There is an evident allusion here to the name Yahweh, the name by which the true God is appropriately designated in the Scriptures. That name Yahweh, from הָיָה, *hayah,* to be, to exist, seems to have been adopted because it denotes

> existence, or being, and as denoting simply one who exists; and has reference merely to the fact of existence. The word has no variation of form, and has no reference to time, and would embrace all time: that is, it is as true at one time as another that he exists. Such a word would not be inappropriately paraphrased by the phrase "who is, and who was, and who is to come," or "who is to be;" and there can be no doubt that John referred to him here as being himself the eternal and uncreated existence, and as the great and original fountain of all being. *Barnes, Albert, Notes on the Bible, 1847-1885, Revelation 1: 4.*
>
> It is evidently on purpose to call attention to the eternity and unchangeableness of God. Used of God in Exo 3:14. *Word Pictures in the New Testament, A.T. Robertson, 1930, Revelation 1:4.*

Who are the "seven spirits" who are before his (Yahweh's) throne? The number seven appears 53 times in Revelation. Seven is symbolic of qualitative completeness or perfection. The seven spirits who stand "before" or "in front of" God's throne represent the complete assembly of heavenly beings who are Yahweh's ministers to the "seven" churches. (Compare Hebrews 1:7,14; Matthew 18:10; 24:31.)

John then mentions "Jesus Christ, the faithful witness, the firstborn from the dead, and the ruler of the kings of the Earth." Jesus completed his mission perfectly. He proclaimed the Kingdom of God; taught and organized his followers to carry on after him; resisted the Devil; maintained his integrity to Yahweh (proved faithful unto death), which allowed the removal of Adam's curse from Adam's offspring; was faithful in everything he did. He was the first one raised from the dead as a spirit endowed with eternal life, and crowned as King of the Messianic Kingdom to rule over the Earth.

> **Revelation 1:8** I am the Alpha and the Omega, says the Lord God, the one who is and the one who was and the one who is coming, the All-Powerful. —*LEB*

As we have seen above, the phrase, "the one who is and the one who was and the one who is coming," refers to Yahweh, the Almighty Creator. This is in harmony with the title, Lord God, as this is a typical replacement in the Septuagint for *Yahweh Elohim*, or *Adonai Yahweh.* (See Genesis 2:8; 15:8.) The Alpha and Omega is Yahweh.

> **I am Alpha and Omega** - These are the first and the last letters of the Greek alphabet, and denote properly the first and the last. . . Among the Jewish rabbis it was common to use the first and the last letters of the Hebrew alphabet to denote the whole of anything, from beginning to end. Thus, it is said, "Adam transgressed the whole law, from 'Aleph (א) to Taw (ת)." "Abraham kept the whole law, from 'Aleph (א) to Taw (ת)." The language here is what would properly denote "eternity" in the being to whom it is applied, and could be used in reference to no one but the true God. It means that he is the beginning and the end of all things; that he was at the commencement, and will be at the close; and it is thus equivalent to saying that he has always existed, and that he will always exist. *Barnes, Albert, Notes on the Bible, 1847-1885, Revelation 1:8.*

Since the title Alpha and Omega implies eternal existence, along with the designation, "the one who is and the one who was and the one who is coming," they cannot apply to Jesus. Jesus was dead for three days (death is the absence of life), therefore he has not been eternal.

> **Revelation 1:17, 18** And when I saw him, I fell at his feet like a dead person, and he placed his right hand on me, saying, "Do not be afraid! I am the first and the last, and the one who lives, and I was dead, and behold, I am living forever and ever, and I hold the keys of death and of Hades." —*LEB*

In John's vision, he sees the exalted Jesus (Revelation 1:13-16), who says in verse 17: "I am the first and the last." This statement is not the same as the Alpha and Omega, which is applied only to Yahweh. Alpha and Omega is a title given to the Lord God by himself, and combined with "the one who is, the one who was, and the one who is coming," denotes eternity and is an allusion to the name, Yahweh. (See Revelation 1:4,5 above.)

The statement by Jesus, "I am the first and the last," denotes something specific to him and him alone. His following words give us a clue to the meaning: "The one who lives, and I was dead, and behold, I am living forever and ever, and I hold the keys of death and Hades." Because of his faithfulness, Jesus was resurrected by Yahweh, and is now living again, this time forever, and he was given authority (the keys) over death and the grave (Hades). By holding the "keys" he will be the one who releases all the human dead from the grave and will eliminate death forever (see Revelation 21:4). This means all other resurrections will be done through him. Therefore, he is the "First" and the "Last," the first human resurrected to an immortal spirit by Yahweh, and the last one resurrected directly by Yahweh. (See Colossians 1:18.)

> **Revelation 3:12** The one who conquers, I will make him a pillar in the temple of my God, and he will never go outside again, and I will write on him the name of my God and the name of the city of my God, the new Jerusalem that comes down from heaven from my God, and my new name. —*LEB*

Jesus is speaking in this verse and admits that, while in heaven as an anointed king, there is one who is above him, who he calls, "my God." The name of his God is Yahweh, the Almighty Creator.

> **Revelation 3:14** "And to the angel of the church in Laodicea write: 'The words of the Amen, the faithful and true witness, the beginning of God's creation.
> —*ESV*

Jesus was created. The *English Standard Version* does not use the original Greek word order. The last phrase can also be translated: "The beginning of the creation of God," as in the *King James Version,* which follows the original word order: ἡ ἀρχὴ τῆς κτίσεως τοῦ θεοῦ, (hey arkhey teys ktĭsey-ōs tou theou).

Like many Greek words, ἀρχὴ (arkhey) has multiple meanings, and arguments have been made that *arkhey* means "ruler" in this verse, which implies Jesus is the Ruler, or Chief of God's creation, or the one who began God's creation. This opinion loses merit when we look at how *arkhey* is used in other verses.

Arkhey is used one other time in relation to Jesus in Colossians 1:18. Here are six different translations of Colossians 1:18:

> He is the beginning *(arkhey)*, the firstborn from the dead, that in everything he might be preeminent.
> —*ESV*

> He is the beginning *(arkhey)*, the firstborn from the dead, so that he himself might have first place in everything. —*ISV*

> Who is the beginning *(arkhey)*, the firstborn from the dead, so that he himself may become first in everything, —*LEB*

> As well as the beginning *(arkhey)*, the firstborn from the dead, so that he himself may become first in all things. —*NET*
>
> For He is the beginning *(arkhey)*, the first-born among the dead, so that He alone should stand first in everything. —*WNT*
>
> He is the first-born Son, who was raised from death, in order that he alone might have the first place in all things. —*GNB*

Notice that even the *Good News Bible,* which re-writes the phrase that includes *arkhey*, still implies a sequential arrangement to the meaning of the verse by stating, “in order that he alone might have the first place in all things.” This is the same meaning in Revelation 3:14. Both verses use a genitive expression, and like every other time *arkhey* appears in the NT followed by a genitive expression, it denotes a beginning or first part of something. (See Mathew 24:8; Mark 13:8,19; John 2:11; Philippians 4:15; Hebrews 5:12;6:1;7:3; 2 Peter 3:4.)

Jesus had a beginning. He was “of creation,” the first part, not the originator, ruler, or overseer. The last clause of Colossians 1:18 emphasizes God’s desire for his son to be “first” in all things: first person created; first heavenly being (*elohim*) to be born as a human; first human to be resurrected as a spirit being; first resurrected being to be granted eternal life; first spirit being to be anointed King over the Earth by Yahweh, the Ancient of Days (Daniel 7:9-14); and given authority to judge the living and the dead.

Chapter 20

Conclusion

In summary:

1. Culture and language both change over time, and the result of those changes have influenced both secular society and theology.

2. The word "God" is consistently a title in Hebrew, Greek, and English, and is applied to many individuals, both heavenly beings and humans. We have also seen that the general quality of a god is essential deity, or being divine, and this is true for the Almighty Creator, all other heavenly beings (both good and bad), and faithful humans who will become sharers in the "divine nature."

3. Being "One with God" does not refer to equality, it refers to unity of purpose, having the same spirit of motivation.

4. Names are important because our reputation is bound to our names. Removing Yahweh's name from scripture dishonors his name.

5. A person called an "Image of God" does not mean that person is equal to God. Being an "Image of God" implies reflecting God's qualities. Adam and Eve were created in the "Image of God," as were heavenly beings (which includes Jesus and the one called Satan the Devil). How well each "Image of God" reflects God's attributes should be judged by the individual, because the ability to manifest God's qualities is not universally equal.

6. The four main characteristics of Yahweh are Love, Wisdom, Power, and Justice. His love for us has restrained his power, to allow time for the issue of universal sovereignty (his right to rule and the willingness of his creation to honor his authority), to be settled. His patience has allowed the Earth to be filled with Adam's offspring, as He commanded while Adam was still in the Garden. His tolerance has allowed the rebellious Sons of God time to prove the accusations raised against Him.

7. Once all the evidence is collected and presented, Yahweh will be justified and the slander spewed by the Accuser Satan, will prove to be empty words. The punishment will fit the crime. For those who choose to reject Yahweh's authority, he will remove them from his Kingdom; They will cease to exist, so those who honor Yahweh's authority can live forever in peace in his Kingdom.

8. Underlying each use of *spirit* is the root understanding of an invisible force (like wind or breath) that can be witnessed and felt, whether an internal (mental) disposition; the force that activates life through breathing; or an external manifestation of power that creates change. There are spirit beings, *elohim* who live in the unseen realm of heaven. There is no *elohim* equal to Yahweh; he is unique among the heavenly beings.

9: Underlying each use of the word *soul* is the reference to the individual being, or each member of a specific class of being. A *soul* needs breath to live. A *soul* can die. *Soul* can be used as a reflexive pronoun, and also indicate the "life" of the individual.

10. All the authors of the writings in the New Testament had the same understanding regarding the Messiah. He was born a perfect man, the equal to Adam; He died as a ransom for Adam's offspring; was resurrected to life by Yahweh, his Father, and exalted to a superior position in heaven than the one he held in his pre-human existence; he was given the gift of immortal life for his faithfulness, and crowned King over humankind.

Knowing the above 10 points are evident in scripture, we should ask, "What led to the changes in Christian doctrine that forsook the original principles and truths in the OT and NT?"

The pagan influence in Modern Christianity is the result of a persistent problem; The same problem that led Israel into apostate worship: pride.

> When pride comes, then comes disgrace, but with the humble is wisdom. *Proverbs 11:2 —ESV*

The unwillingness to put off pagan traditions and adhere to God's will, quickly corrupted the Christian church. This apostasy began in the first-century.

> But even in the apostolic age many Jews and Gentiles were baptized only with water, not with the Holy Spirit and fire of the gospel, and smuggled their old religious notions and practices into the church. Hence the heretical tendencies, which are combated in the New Testament, especially in the Pauline and Catholic Epistles. *Schaff, Philip, 1890, History Of The Christian Church, 5th Edition, The Complete Eight Volumes In One, page 928, Kindle Edition.*

Philip Schaff's assessment regarding the theological corruption is proven true by statements written in the following scriptures.

> As I urged you when I was leaving for Macedonia, stay on in Ephesus to instruct certain people not to spread false teachings, nor to occupy themselves with myths and interminable genealogies. Such things promote useless speculations rather than God's redemptive plan that operates by faith. But the aim of our instruction is love that comes from a pure heart, a good conscience, and a sincere faith. Some have strayed from these and turned away to empty discussion. They want to be teachers of the law, but they do not understand what they are

saying or the things they insist on so confidently. *—1 Timothy 1:3-7 NET*

Make every effort to present yourself approved to God, a worker having no need to be ashamed, guiding the word of truth along a straight path. But avoid pointless chatter, for it will progress to greater ungodliness, and their message will spread like gangrene, among whom are Hymenaeus and Philetus, who have deviated concerning the truth by saying the resurrection has already taken place, and they are upsetting the faith of some. *—2 Timothy 2:15-19 LEB*

But now, because you have come to know God, or rather have come to be known by God, how can you turn back again to the weak and miserable elemental spirits? Do you want to be enslaved to them all over again? You carefully observe days and months and seasons and years. I am afraid for you, lest perhaps I have labored for you in vain! *—Galatians 4:9-11 LEB*

And regard the patience of our Lord as salvation, just as also our dear brother Paul wrote to you, according to the wisdom that was given to him, as he does also in all his letters, speaking in them about these things, in which there are some things hard to understand, which the ignorant and unstable distort to their own destruction, as they also do the rest of the scriptures. *—2 Peter 3:15,16 LEB*

For there are many rebellious people, idle talkers, and deceivers, especially those with Jewish

> connections, who must be silenced because they mislead whole families by teaching for dishonest gain what ought not to be taught. A certain one of them, in fact, one of their own prophets, said, "Cretans are always liars, evil beasts, lazy gluttons." Such testimony is true. For this reason, rebuke them sharply that they may be healthy in the faith and not pay attention to Jewish myths and commands of people who reject the truth. All is pure to those who are pure. But to those who are corrupt and unbelieving, nothing is pure, but both their minds and consciences are corrupted. They profess to know God but with their deeds they deny him, since they are detestable, disobedient, and unfit for any good deed. *—Titus 1:10-16 NET*

Paul foretold the apostasy would continue into the future.

> For the mystery of lawlessness is already at work, but the one who now restrains will do so until he is taken out of the way. And then the lawless one will be revealed, whom the Lord will destroy with the breath of his mouth and annihilate by the appearance of his coming. The coming of the lawless one will be in accordance with the working of Satan, with all kinds of counterfeit miracles, signs, and wonders, and with every kind of wicked deception among those who are perishing, because they refused to love the truth and so be saved. For this reason, God will send them a powerful delusion, leading them to believe what is false, so that all who have not believed the truth but have taken pleasure in unrighteousness will be condemned. *—2 Thessalonians 2:7-12 TCENT*

The apostles and disciples of Jesus were not taught to spread a new religion. They were taught and commanded to spread the Good News of the Kingdom of God (see Matthew 24:14). The God of Israel, Yahweh, was still their God. Only the need for the Mosaic Law changed (see Galatians 3:15-29). The Law was made obsolete by Christ's sacrificial death, and this was made obvious to the world in 70 C.E. when the Jerusalem Temple was demolished stone by stone (compare Matthew 24:1,2). The redemption of humankind, through faith in the ransom supplied by the death of the Messiah, and not through animal sacrifice, made the Law of Moses unnecessary. (See Hebrews 9:1-28.)

As time passed and the Good News spread around the Mediterranean, corrupt humans began molding the faith into something more pleasing to themselves; something they could use to gain authority over others.

> For the time is coming when people will not endure sound teaching, but having itching ears they will accumulate for themselves teachers to suit their own passions, and will turn away from listening to the truth and wander off into myths. —2 Timothy 4:3,4 ESV

The division between Laity and Clergy was eventually born, contrary to the standard set by Jesus and the Apostles of a brotherhood. The result is what we have today: multiple Christian denominations with human leaders. (Compare Matthew 23:1-13; Romans 16:17,18; Galatians 3:28.)

During the centuries after the apostles died, the human leaders of the apostate Christian church continued to hide the proper name of God, and applied Greek understanding to the scriptures. This led to Jesus becoming God Almighty in their minds, and caused Yahweh to shrink into obscurity as the Father. With the creation of the equally obscure Holy Ghost, a nameless deity without form, a pagan trinity of gods was born.

While Jesus is the focus of the New Testament, nowhere in the text is he viewed as equal to Yahweh by the authors. If the Apostles understood Jesus to be God Almighty, then in the Book of Acts what message would they have proclaimed? Would we not shout from the mountain tops that Almighty God had been here on Earth with us! Yet nowhere in Acts do we find expressions stating Jesus was God Almighty. We find expressions about his death, his resurrection (by God), and the need to have faith in his sacrificial ransom, but nothing that elevates him to equality with Yahweh. To the authors of the New Testament Jesus is the Messiah, who was exalted by Yahweh to a superior position in heaven for his faithfulness (See Philippians 2: 8-11.)

Since the Council of Chalcedon in 451 C.E. (see End Note 2), when the Triune Godhead was cemented into Christian orthodoxy, the Good News has been hijacked by false prophets, and the truth about Jesus concealed by corrupt theologians. Over 400 years after Jesus was crucified, the religion that claimed to follow his teachings followed instead doctrines that were never proclaimed by Jesus or any other prophet of Yahweh; They embraced a lie. Since then, they continue to twist the scriptures to prove their false doctrines are God-Inspired.

Knowing the possibilities the future held, Jesus told his apostles the Parable of the Persistent Widow:

> Then Jesus told them a parable to show them they should always pray and not lose heart. He said, “In a certain city there was a judge who neither feared God nor respected people. There was also a widow in that city who kept coming to him and saying, ‘Give me justice against my adversary.’ For a while he refused, but later on he said to himself, ‘Though I neither fear God nor have regard for people, yet because this widow keeps on bothering me, I will give her justice, or in the end she will wear me out by her unending pleas.’”

> And the Lord said, "Listen to what the unrighteous judge says! Won't God give justice to his chosen ones, who cry out to him day and night? Will he delay long to help them? I tell you; he will give them justice speedily. Nevertheless, when the Son of Man comes, will he find faith on earth?" *—Luke 18:1-8 NET*

Will he find faith on Earth? Those calling, "Lord, Lord," believe they are doing what is right, and yet Jesus tells them, "I never knew you. Depart from me, you who practice lawlessness!'" (See Matthew 7:21-23)

One undeniable trait in humans has been manifest since Adam's rejection of Yahweh's authority: selfish desire—the one internal obstacle that stifles spiritual growth. That trait, combined with the corrupting influence from wicked spirits, has led humankind to the precipice of complete disaster.

And yet, despite the horrible results of Adam's lawless attitude, Yahweh still desires all of us grab hold of the saving grace he has made available through his son. All it takes on our part is to acknowledge the undeserved kindness of the offer, and accept the ransom of Jesus' perfect human life in exchange for the life that Adam forfeited.

> But as many as received him—to those who believe in his name—he gave to them authority to become children of God. *—John 1:12 LEB*

End Notes

1. Pagan Trinities

Samaria: Anu - Enlil – Ea

“The universe was divided into three regions each of which became the domain of a god. Anu's share was the sky. The earth was given to Enlil. Ea became the ruler of the waters. Together they constituted the triad of the Great Gods.” *The Larousse Encyclopedia of Mythology, 1994, pp.54-55.*

Babylon: Enki - Tammuz - Ishtar

“The ancient Babylonians recognized the doctrine of a trinity, or three persons in one god—as appears from a composite god with three heads forming part of their mythology, and the use of the equilateral triangle, also, as an emblem of such trinity in unity.” *Rock, Thomas Dennis, 1867, The Mystical Woman and the Cities of the Nations, pp. 22 23.*

India: Shiva - Vishnu - Brahma

"The Puranas, one of the Hindu Bibles of more than 3,000 years ago, contain the following passage: 'O ye three Lords! know that I recognize only one God. Inform me, therefore, which of you is the true divinity, that I may address to him alone my adorations.' The three gods, Brahma, Vishnu, and Siva [or Shiva], becoming manifest to him, replied, 'Learn, O devotee, that there is no real distinction between us. What to you appears such is only the semblance. The single being appears under three forms by the acts of creation, preservation, and destruction, but he is one.'
"Hence the triangle was adopted by all the ancient nations as a symbol of the Deity . . . Three was considered among all the pagan nations as the chief of the mystical numbers, because, as Aristotle remarks, it contains within itself a beginning, a middle, and an end. Hence we find it designating some of the attributes of almost all the pagan gods." *Sinclair, Maria, 1876, Old Truths in a New Light, pp. 382-383.*

Greece: Zeus - Athene - Apollo

"In the Fourth-Century B.C. Aristotle wrote: 'All things are three, and thrice is all: and let us use this number in the worship of the gods; for, as the Pythagoreans say, everything and all things are bounded by threes, for the end, the middle and the beginning have this number in everything, and these compose the number of the Trinity.'" *Weigall, Arthur, 1928, Paganism in Our Christianity, pp. 197-198.*

Egypt: Amun - Re - Ptah

"The Hymn to Amun decreed that 'No god came into being before him (Amun)' and that 'All gods are three: Amun, Re and Ptah, and there is no second to them. Hidden is his name as Amon, he is Re in face, and his body is Ptah.' . . . This is a statement of trinity, the three chief gods of

Egypt subsumed into one of them, Amon. Clearly, the concept of organic unity within plurality got an extraordinary boost with this formulation. Theologically, in a crude form it came strikingly close to the later Christian form of plural Trinitarian monotheism." *Najovits, Simson, 2004, Egypt, Trunk of the Tree, Vol. 2, pp. 83-84*

2. Council of Chalcedon

Council of Chalcedon, fourth ecumenical council of the Christian church, held in Chalcedon (modern Kadiköy, Turkey) in 451. Convoked by the emperor Marcian, it was attended by about 520 bishops or their representatives and was the largest and best documented of the early councils. It approved the creed of Nicaea (325), the creed of Constantinople (381; subsequently known as the Nicene Creed), two letters of St. Cyril of Alexandria against Nestorius, which insisted on the unity of divine and human persons in Christ, and the Tome of Pope Leo I confirming two distinct natures in Christ and rejecting the Monophysite doctrine that Christ had only one nature. The council then explained these doctrines in its own confession of faith.

Besides reinforcing canons of earlier church councils as well as declarations of some local synods, the council issued disciplinary decrees affecting monks and clergy and declared Jerusalem and Constantinople patriarchates. The overall effect was to give the church a more stable institutional character.

Britannica, The Editors of Encyclopedia. "Council of Chalcedon," Encyclopedia Britannica, 24 Jul. 2019, https://www.britannica.com/event/Council-of-Chalcedon

Acknowledgements:

This work would not have been possible without the help of Frank S., Zee, Debbie E., Kimberly V., and so many others whose faith and persistence helped move this project across the finish line.

May the glory go the the Father, whose loyal love is everlasting. Praise Yah!

About the Author:

P.D. Blackwell is a lifelong student who began studying theology, religion, and physics in 1980. He practices the guitar and piano every day, and enjoys a good game of chess.

www.ingramcontent.com/pod-product-compliance
Lightning Source LLC
LaVergne TN
LVHW050640100826
845148LV00011B/1928

* 9 7 8 1 7 3 6 6 0 9 6 3 7 *